NAKED NOMADS
Unmarried Men in America

Books by George Gilder

The Party That Lost Its Head
(co-authored with Bruce Chapman)

Sexual Suicide

NAKED NOMADS
Unmarried Men in America

George Gilder

Quadrangle/The New York Times Book Co.

Library of Congress Cataloging in Publication Data

Gilder, George F   1939–
   Naked nomads.

   1. Bachelors. 2. Divorcees. I. Title.
HQ800.G48 1974   301.41'76'422   74-79945
ISBN 0-8129-0495-8

39340

To David and Peggy

Acknowledgments

I would like to begin by acknowledging a writer and friend, Kerry Gruson, who had nothing specific to do with anything in this book but whose struggle for life, carried on while I wrote it, triumphed with a grace and beauty that excel any possible attainment of art.

The primary acknowledgment must go to all those women whose incredible restraint and forbearance have allowed me to remain single long enough to research and finish this book. They have saved me from a likely career of writing about international economics, Republican politics, and other matters somehow less stirring than the "naked nomads" and "sexual suicides" to whom I have resorted in my single predicament.

Nonetheless, there are many others who must share the credit and the blame for this book. For my style—whatever virtues it may have—I must implicate Joan Didion, since I spent much of my time reabsorbing all her works before I began writing mine. *Slouching Towards Bethlehem* yields me new miracles every time I read it, which is about four times a year.

Ortega y Gasset and Walter Lippmann taught me how to think and Margaret Mead taught me how to think about the sexes. The music and rhythm came chiefly from Charles Mingus and my mother. The confidence to write narrative prose and dialogue came from Edgar Rosenberg. Wherever he may be, I hope his students appreciate him more than Harvard did.

Because this book had to be finished quickly, its numerous editors must share an unusual proportion of the credit or blame for transforming it from a pig's ear of *Sexual Suicide* into its currently silken prose—or whatever. The key professional editors were Carol Southern and Susan Arensberg.

Carol was diligent, balanced, and intelligent and refused to take any guff, no matter how loudly I oinked. Susan has worked on three of my books now and I hope she will edit all the rest.

Then there were the amateur editors. Every writer should have someone like Michael Padnos read his book. But as anyone who knows him will affirm, there *is* no one like Michael Padnos. In this case, he was the mad slasher, and after he overcame his initial impulse to cut the entire book, he gave brilliant and excisive advice on several chapters.

Nelson Aldrich, Jr., of *Harper's* gave me wise and sympathetic counsel for the entire year between the publication of *Sexual Suicide* and this book and heavily contributed to its point of view. Robert Grymes and Arthur Norton of the Census Bureau gave me generous and intelligent assistance with the statistics.

Michael Brewer, who never lets his job or other distractions prevent him from helping a friend, continually alerted me to valuable research materials and was never too tired or busy to debate my arguments.

Anne Hebald gave the book an especially useful reading, detecting a large number of the tics, conceits, and obscurities that cluttered my prose. The first reader of the book was David Quattrone, who gave me a crucial early sense of where to focus my rewriting. Louise Fisher did much of the typing with cool, professional dispatch despite pressures of time, heat, and my bad penmanship.

Herbert Nagourney of Quadrangle was as direct, honest, and decisive as ever, and in a real sense this book is his, since it was his confidence and support that made its writing and publication possible.

I hope all the losing participants in the title debate will forgive me my final choice.

George F. Gilder
Tyringham, Mass.
July 15, 1974

Contents

PROLOGUE	Inspecting the Rocks	1
1	Single Man Blues	8
2	The Death of a Single Man	22
3	The Divorce Losers	29
4	Lennie and Frank at "Love Unlimited"	42
5	Revolutionary Hayrides	56
6	Single Menace	67
7	Immaculate Evolution	81
8	A Man and His Body	92
9	Rights of the Knife	106
10	Jobs Without Gender	123
11	How Love Works	133
12	Why Men Marry	147
EPILOGUE	The Nudist on the Beach	160
	Notes	163
	Index	177

NAKED NOMADS
Unmarried Men in America

Prologue

Inspecting the Rocks

I was walking on the road, a dusty road just like the one at home. On both sides of the road were trees. They stood tall and thick as far as they went. I was walking on this dusty road; really, with most of my toes bleeding, I was hobbling. Once in a while I would look back at my footprints, and I would grieve to myself that these footprints would soon be washed away by the water of rain, or they would soon be swept away by the broom of wind, and more grieving was the thought that my mother would never come here and see these footprints and say, "I know who passed here." . . .

To one who has taken to wandering from place to place, from country to country . . . a good living once established survives only until the impulse to wandering revives . . . a stranded man such as I departs and strikes once more for the distant destination.

—LEGSON KAYIRA

I am writing this from a hospital on a small French island in the Caribbean three thousand miles from home. The nurse is efficient but she does not speak the kind of French I understand—slow French, Edith Piaf French, prep school *français*—but rather some argot that would remind me of my last time in Montreal—if I had ever been to Montreal. (My mind does wander, but it is still there.) When she glances at me, her eyes flash distress and turn away. Nurses should learn not to do that. (It is only my face that may be gone.)

1

Seventeen hours ago I paused briefly to look at the view from a small cliff above a rocky beach. I planned to lie in the sun on a flat space ten feet below. Though I did not have much time to relax, I did want to get a handsome tan before I left the island. After all, I am a single man.

Perhaps you know the view—the intense blue sky, the darker blue sea, the sails on the horizon, the crash and spume of waves below on the rocks—the kind of view that makes one feel one could ride the breezes above it with the terns. Then off to the left there was a pelican. A ridiculous contraption of a bird, it was selected by nature for its huge beak and gorge, which it uses to scoop up little fish from the tides. It is gobbling one now . . . gulp. If a scarecrow could eat fish, it would swallow them like a pelican. For all our hairless lumpiness, I thought, humans are elegant in comparison. But watch . . . It is a bird, and it rises to the occasion of the view. Spreading its huge wings and sweeping lithely along above the water before plummeting on a line into the surf, it is beautiful. With a face like that, I thought, it had had to learn to do something.

Then I fell to the rocks below. I don't know how it happened. There was no warning whatsoever. Something slipped. I suppose that is the way these things normally happen. One day the car does not pull out of the skid. Or a brick is dislodged from the side of a building above. Or the mugger is offended. This time I found myself falling. I was in a dive head first, ten feet through the air, splat . . . into unconsciousness . . . and out the other side, rising up in a cold scalding stew of blood and skin and terror. This is what it is like to die, I thought. But it did not seem to be an artery or a broken neck, and my legs were there, yes, and through the spume, I could still somewhat see, and my arms worked. I pressed a towel against my face and ran up the hill from the rocks, startling some workmen, and stumbled up to the house, there was so much blood and pain, and rushed headlong to the nearest mirror.

I was very interested, as I remember, in what had happened to my nose. But when I looked in the mirror, there was just a smear of blood and crumbled rock. I walked over to my bed and lay back on it with the towel still across my face. People began to gather. They seemed to know who I was. I was not sure. Identity is fed by love. How can one be loved with a scarred and broken face? What pelican tricks could I learn—endearing comic touches or poetic flights—to redeem my misshapen beak?

There were two good moments, though. A lovely French girl, working as a maid and serving me meals, washed some of the carnage from my face and looked into it with tender concern. Then Monsieur Salazar came. The caretaker of the place I was visiting, he had stayed the course as a soldier through three French wars. Then he had rebelled with General Salan against De Gaulle after the troops were withdrawn from Algeria. De Gaulle had sent him to prison for two years. Mine was not the first bashed face that Monsieur Salazar had seen. He looked at it and lent it dignity, connecting it briefly with all the others—the young Frenchmen from whose wounds had flowed the blood of the French empire as it expired. "Ah, *un blessé de guerre,*" he said. Something on my face tried to smile. I was looking for glamor anywhere I could find it. But somehow I knew I could not remain in the company of French war heroes. *"Un blessé de soleil,"* I said.

The doctors came and I was taken by boat to the hospital. I was extraordinarily lucky. Somehow I had fallen ten feet onto solid rock and landed directly on my nose and forehead without a serious concussion or any major fractures. My nose had been broken, my forehead gouged, and there was a half circle of gashes surrounding my left eye where my steel glasses had been. The whole mess had swollen to a ridiculous size and I could not open the eye. The next day, however, with all the stitches, and the crevices to see through, I looked no worse than Carmen Basilio after his very most disastrous fight—or one of those other remorseless white boxers who sometimes win by blocking punches with their faces all night long. I was reassured to think that they recover; and women love them, perhaps not only for their money. Perhaps I would not have to be single for the rest of my life.

This was of some concern to me because I was on the island to write this book, and I knew all too much about the lives of single men. In the chapter I wrote the day before my injury, for example, I had disclosed that single men are six times more likely than married ones to die from "accidental falls." I knew that in a real sense my tumble was no accident, that from the Olympian view of the sociologist or of the man at the National Center for Health Statistics, my fall was not improbable. A car accident would have been more likely. But single men, in some deep way, place less value on their lives, are more careless with them than married men or single women.

We make our way through the rocks and high places, balancing our pitcher of blood, without stays to family or children, past or future, untied and free. When we waver, there is no balancing wire; when we fall, we fall alone. We are useful in wars, and mobs. We make good saints and martyrs, good fanatics and racing car drivers, good criminals and Green Berets, geniuses and psychopaths. But unless we finally fall into marriage, we are likely to fall on the rocks.

You do not believe me. You think I am melodramatic. That is because you have not been inspecting the rocks. Why are there so many single men there? Why do single men head every index of failure and disease, crime and disruption?

That is the riddle with which I began this book. It is ultimately unanswerable, because it contains the enigma of cause and effect, chicken and egg. It is impossible to finally determine to what extent single men are single because they are in some sense flawed, and to what extent they are flawed because they are single. I believe, however, that singleness is to a great extent the cause—that single men are in trouble because they are single and the single life is destructive to men. I do not have proof. My case is largely circumstantial, atmospheric, speculative.

For the basic facts of the single man's predicament, I begin on the rocks, at the Bureau of the Census and the National Center for Health Statistics. Then I proceed to my own life, and the lives of unmarried friends and acquaintances. I consult biology, anthropology, and economics. There are still no final answers. All we know for certain is that in the generations of single men, most get married and they change, while some stay single and they tend rapidly to deteriorate. We know that single women do not similarly decline. And we know that the single existence falls far short of its notices.

*   *   *

The best comment on the singles life—made in the face of all the propaganda for its charms—comes from the singles themselves: They are getting married faster than ever before in history. The median age of marriage is only twenty-three for men and twenty-one for women, just a slight rise over previous levels.

Most young people avoid being single as much as possible. During the last ten years the marriage rate, adjusted for age and population, increased by 26 percent. Between 1970 and 1973 the number of married couples increased by 1,543,-000 and now nearly 80 percent of American households consist of intact families.[1] Of course, people are also getting divorced faster than ever, and the divorce rate in 1971 passed the record set during the period after World War II.[2] But even so, between 1970 and 1973, there were three times as many marriages as divorces.[3] And even the divorces do not seem to suggest any enthusiasm for being single. The first thing many people do after breaking up is to get remarried. The remarriage rate went up by 40 percent during the decade up to 1973.[4]

Nor are the odds against current marriages, unless they occur between teenagers. Census bureau experts predict that only one in six marriages begun now between white individuals over twenty-one will end in divorce.[5] And, finally, in 1970—after all these years of singles celebration and of women moving in and out of the job force—68 percent believed that "taking care of a home and family" was more interesting than having a job. This proportion is up 18 percent since 1946.[6] Although these figures came before women's liberation reached its peak of publicity, there is little evidence in more recent data that a significantly higher proportion of women are rejecting marriage.

People continue to vote with their feet against the singles life. It is important to understand why. An appreciation of the futility of a singles pattern for people of all ages beyond the early twenties can be the beginning of wisdom about human life itself. Understanding the failure of the singles style, one can comprehend the real potentialities and limits of men and women, the real possibilities for freedom and the real needs for dependency and responsibility. One can explain the barrenness of much of our popular culture and the shallowness of much of our most highly sophisticated literature and cinema. One can gain a deeper perspective on the breakdown of many of our government's social programs.

The failure of the singles ideal is a major sociological fact of the last decade. Many more publicized developments are related to this failure. Yet it is still to be studied. Census figures by marital status are inadequate. Few government agencies assemble statistics on singles life. But the statistics as they emerge are devastating.

The key to the failure is not, as often supposed, the insistent need of women for marriage. Although they may make claims to the contrary, women, in fact, can often do without marriage; single women at least can live to a stable and productive old age. The key to the singles failure is the profound biological dependence of men on women—deeper than any feminist or male chauvinist understands. Men without women frequently become the "single menace" and tend to live short and destructive lives—destructive both to themselves and to the society.

Our major social problem thus comes from single men, the very people who have apparently best achieved the national ideal of independence and freedom. The most liberated Americans are also the most afflicted—and afflictive. Our problem in the United States seems to be that we are getting what we want. Perhaps that indicates something important about our current social ideals.

1

Single Man Blues

It is a truth universally acknowledged that a single man in possession of a good fortune must be in want of a wife.
—JANE AUSTEN

I know of no medicine fit to diminish the violent natural inclinations you mention and if I did, I think I should not communicate it to you. Marriage is the proper remedy, the natural state of a man. A single man has not nearly the value he would have in the State of Union. He is an incomplete man, the odd half of a pair of scissors.
—BENJAMIN FRANKLIN
A Letter to a Young Man on Taking a Mistress

The single man. An image of freedom and power. A man on horseback, riding into the sunset with his gun. The town and its women would never forget, never be the same. But the man would never change, just move on. To other women, other towns. As he rides away, the sunset gives him a romantic glow.

The single man. The naked nomad in the bedrooms of the land. The celebrity at the party, combed by eyes of envy and desire. The hero of film and television drama: cool, violent, sensuous, fugitive, *free*.

The American dream, the Superstar: If one were only rich, young, famous, one would revel as a single man. One would be—Namath? Dylan? McCartney? George Plimpton? Jay Rockefeller? Dick Cavett? Mick Jagger? Jean Claude Killy? O. J. Simpson?

In fact, if one were young, rich, and famous, one most likely would be—as every society hostess learns when she seeks "eligible" escorts for the successful single women at her parties—one would be a married man. Of the listed celebrities, only Namath is still single.

Then there is Joe Quarterman to sum it all up in song. Quarterman, who aspires to be the next James Brown, spends much of his time conveying a sense of sexual come-and-get it: He wants every female body in the room, *right now,* splayed, on the stage. After his performances, which feature such works as "I'm Gonna Get You" . . . "I've been watching you, I've gotta have you"—and which often climax with "Gimme, Gimme, Gimme . . . Uh! . . . Back My Freedom," the phone numbers patter around him like snow. Everything about the public Joe Quarterman evokes the imagery of the high-cruising, easy-riding, liberated single male.

Yet, remember, Joe Quarterman wants to be the new James Brown. Like the old James Brown, he is not one to be snowed by phone numbers. Joe Quarterman always goes home to his wife and two children: "This woman is one hundred percent in my corner," he says. So Joe Quarterman is becoming a success.[1] That is the way it usually is with our successful purveyors of the single ideal. Singleness is a nice place to visit, but you wouldn't want to live there.

If, on the other hand, one were actually a single man, unattached—free in the spirit of our Mediated dream, our memory of youth that improves with age, our love 'em and leave 'em Lancelot, our easy-riding ranger—one would be . . . ? Well, we know from the statistics: The single man in general, compared to others in the population, is poor and neurotic. He is disposed to criminality, drugs, and violence. He is irresponsible about his debts, alcoholic, accident prone, and venereally diseased. Unless he can marry, he is often destined to a Hobbsean life—solitary, poor, nasty, brutish, and short—the kind of life that led Hobbsean man to form a new social contract. It leads modern man to get married.

Of course, there are many exceptions. One must expect a barrage of indignant testimony from the single men who ostensibly violate the pattern of irresponsibility and neurosis. One will hear about former prime minister Heath, and former prime bachelor Pierre Elliott Trudeau. One will even be flattered with observations about oneself. I am admittedly yet to be arrested for violent crime or alcoholism. Despite general encouragement from book reviewers and other telepathic diagnosticians, I am yet to be put away for mental illness. There is no doubt that millions of single men have managed to become disciplined and valuable citizens, and millions of divorced men have survived to a happy and productive old age.

In addition, bachelors form a fluid group. Every man is single at least for a while. Many men are divorced or widowed. Millions are merely temporary bachelors looking for a wife. Most will eventually find one. Some will not, but will spend their lives in the quest. An indeterminate number are homosexuals. Even some of them will marry.

One might expect men so diverse to defy generalization. What could the football star have in common with the transvestite singer? How can the bachelor playboy, too frivolous to marry, resemble the young executive, too busy to marry? What characteristics can the older divorced man share with the young graduate student—or the middle-aged philanthropist share with the ghetto pusher or the flower child? How can a young man on the way to marriage resemble an old man who never married?

The answer may be deceptively obvious: all bachelors lack wives. This lack is more important in some ways than all the apparent differences among single men in age, wealth, class, culture, and status.

The statistics are overwhelming. One can easily identify a bachelor pattern. It is marked by lack of sustained commitment and lack of orientation toward the future. The single man tends to move from one sexual partner to another, from job to job, city to city, rotating his life without growth or progress. And when a man gets divorced or widowed, he tends to revert in many respects to the temperament of the never-married single man.

Underlying all the superficial diversity of bachelor life is a syndrome of psychological instability. In a sense, the bachelor may never grow up. Thus the older unmarried man in many ways may resemble the young man, unless he acquires direct dependents and responsibilities. The homosexual may display a pattern of neurosis quite similar to the pattern of other committed bachelors. All, under the garments of culture, may be naked nomads, lacking roots in the past and connections to the future. And the erratic and impulsive course of the single man, however attractive among the young, becomes pathological as a man grows older unmarried.

One striking aspect of the bachelor pattern is low income. Because of their tendency toward mental instability, physical disease, and early mortality, single men earn less over their lifetime than any other major category of workers. Although discrimination is not a serious problem for white bachelors, they make no higher yearly incomes, on the average, than such official victims of bias as married blacks and single women.

In economic terms, the group most representative of the single male condition is never-married bachelors between the ages of twenty-five and sixty-five. The incomes of the divorced and widowed benefit from their time as married men, while the figures for single men below twenty-five are distorted by schooling commitments. In addition, the young men are getting married so fast that it is difficult to sort out the real bachelors from those just passing through on the way to church.

Excluding the divorced and widowed, there are a little over 4,000,000 single men between twenty-five and sixty-five.[2] About 7 percent are inmates in correctional or mental institutions.[3] This leaves about 3,650,000 on the loose. Of these, about 330,000 are unemployed or unregistered in the labor force, [4] leaving 3,320,000 single men at work. They do not tend to work very hard, however. Only a little more than 60 percent were on the job full time—a little higher than single women but about 20 percent behind married men.[5]

In general, the 3,320,000 single male workers hardly earned enough to feed themselves and buy *Playboy,* let alone follow its philosophy. In 1970, their average income was approximately 6,000 dollars, their median income 5,800 [6] (a median means half are above and half below).

Singleness correlates with poverty better than race does. One way to explain black poverty is to point out that 39 percent of black men are single, compared to 27 percent of whites.[7] Outside the South, married black males under thirty-five earn about 30 percent more than comparable white singles.[8]

Although it may be hard to believe, in view of the feminist outcry, single men earn about the same as single women of the same age and qualifications. Between the ages of thirty and forty-four, according to a Labor Department study, both earn about the same hourly wages.[9] Under age fifty-five, the single men work more hours than single women and earn a little more. After age fifty-five, the average incomes of single women edge above those of single men.[10] Single college graduates over age twenty-five earn about the same amount, whether male or female. Both earned a median income of approximately 9,500 dollars in 1972.[11]

Married men, however, earned nearly twice as much as singles of either sex. Between the ages of forty-five and fifty-four, for example, single white men with college degrees earn an average of about 10,500 dollars. Married men earn about 19,000.[12] Single college graduates earn about the same as married high school graduates. In addition, the married high school graduate has a nearly four times better chance than a comparable single of eventually earning over 15,000 dollars.[13] It would seem more important for an ambitious young single man to get married than to go to college.

When the low incomes of single men are noticed at all, they are often attributed to "discrimination." The singles magazines would have us add single men to the current list of bias victims, eligible to benefit from the "affirmative action" and anti-discrimination rulings of the federal government. The Equal Employment Opportunities Commission (EEOC) already tends to assume that any group earning less than others of the same age and measurable qualifications must be a victim of bias.

Earnings, however, are not determined by measurable characteristics such as education and "intelligence." Studies by M.I.T. economist Lester Thurow[14] and sociologist Christopher Jencks[15] have shown that the keys to a worker's productivity and earning power are such incalculable qualities as motivation, diligence, drive, competitiveness, leadership, initiative, regularity, mobility, and luck. Men earn most if they compete hard, demand high salaries, and are willing to move if they do not get them. Thurow has also demonstrated that on-the-job training is much more productive than college.

To decide employment status chiefly on the basis of education or "intelligence" is merely to discriminate against the high school graduate with an intense drive to get ahead and a large family to support. It is also, incidentally, to discriminate against the business with realistic and intelligent personnel policies, free of class and educationist bias. Most businesses know that single men, regardless of their intelligence and credentials, tend to be less stable and resolute workers than married men. Married men are the only ones in the population that are a great success at earning money. In general, married men need money more than women or single men, so they tend to fight for it and get it.

Although single men make no more money than women, who are said to be gravely victimized by bias, "discrimination" is not the bachelor's problem. His chief problem is his own psychological and physical condition. He is his own worst enemy.

In general, men have more psychological problems than women, and single men have the most problems of all. Much of the relevant data, ironically, was presented two years ago by Phyllis Chesler in her best-selling book *Women and Madness*.[16] Although she shows that women constitute 52 percent of the "psychiatrically involved," [17] women constitute about 54 percent of the adult population. Proportionately, therefore, men are more heavily represented.

In addition, nowhere in the 1970 U.S. census volume on *Persons in Institutions and Other Group Quarters* (including data from all mental hospitals and residential treatment centers, public and private) is there any evidence that women comprise more than about 44 percent of those sufficiently sick to be institutionalized. The figure would be about 40 percent without the large number of elderly women over sixty-five.[18]

Many mentally disturbed persons are not incarcerated in mental hospitals. In all institutions, including prisons, hospitals, and old age homes, as well as mental facilities, men comprise more than 53 percent of the inmate populations. Their *median* age is 47.3 compared to 75.1(!) for the women. Below age sixty-five, institutionalized men outnumber women about three to one.[19]

Another valuable index of mental health are the statistics on psychiatric outpatients (not institutionalized). Chesler's figures on the marital status of psychiatric outpatients (Table 8) suggest that between ages eighteen and sixty-four about 14 percent more white women than men go to psychiatrists.

The table shows that single women have a rate (as outpatients) well over twice as high as married women. The table also indicates—in accord with much other evidence—that divorced *men* have the highest outpatient rate of all. And the table shows that single men have a higher rate than any group except the divorced—a fact also confirmed by other sources.[20] For both sexes, but most particularly for men, singleness and liberation seem to be conditions of mental illness.

Visits to psychiatrists are only one index of the condition of these unattached men. Sociologist Jessie Bernard has assembled much material indicating that single men are far more prone to mental and physical disorders than any other large group of Americans, with the possible exception of the divorced.[21]

She also shows that the longer they stay single the worse they get. Thus, according to data collected in 1968 by the National Center for Health Statistics, approximately 92 percent of both single and married men between the ages of seventeen and forty-four were free of chronic physical disorders. After age forty-five, however, only 73 percent of the single men were found to be free of disorders, where as 82 percent of the married men were still healthy. This means that more than one quarter of all single men between forty-five and sixty-five apparently have some chronic physical disorder restricting their activity.[22]

Surveys studying clinical depression in married and single men present similar findings: The symptoms do not manifest themselves until after age forty-five. It would seem, therefore, that it is not the symptoms that prevent singles from getting married but that prolonged singleness may cause the symptoms.[23]

Of course, all such statistics are affected by late marriages that move the undepressed and healthy singles from the unmarried to the married column, leaving the worst cases in the singles total. But first marriages are very rare after forty. And in any case, they are counteracted in the figures by the death rate. The death rate of late middle age singles is more than twice as high as the marriage rate and twice as high as the death rate of married men. Thus the data showing late development of symptoms by singles is not a statistical illusion.[24]

There is no question that even beyond major depression and chronic disease conditions, the group of single men between twenty-five and sixty-five is in bad shape psychologically. Other Bernard tables show they are over 30 percent more likely than married men or single women to be depressed; 30 percent more likely to show "phobic tendencies" and "passivity"; and almost twice as likely to show "severe neurotic symptoms." They are almost three times as prone to nervous breakdowns. They can't sleep (three times more insomnia) and if they do sleep they are three times more likely to have nightmares.[25] Several surveys from diverse communities comparing them to married men indicate that they have only between one fourth and one half as good a chance of considering themselves happy.[26]

Perhaps the most striking findings presented by Ms. Bernard come from a study by Leo Srole and associates, *Mental Health in the Metropolis, The Midtown Manhattan Study*.[27] Srole's report found that married men and women do not greatly differ in their mental health. About one fifth of both are impaired. In this survey, unlike some others, single women are slightly better off. But like all of the available data, the report finds single men in the worst condition and deteriorating most rapidly with age. Between the ages of fifty and fifty-nine, an astonishing total of 46.1 percent of all single men in the Manhattan survey show "mental health impairment." [28] Again it seems that singleness itself is the culprit.

Particularly in big cities, many single men are homosexuals. Although the precise number cannot be determined, it is likely that as much as a quarter of the single male sample is gay. The effect on the statistics, however, is much smaller than might be expected. In their pattern of afflictions, male homosexuals resemble other single men.

The chief difference, of course, is in sexual experience. A recent study by the (Kinsey) Institute for Sex Research indicates that homosexuals claim to be happier and to get much more sex than most other single men.[29] According to the figures, almost 60 percent of all homosexuals have sex more than once a week and 22 percent have sex three times a week or more. More than two thirds of homosexuals are currently promiscuous (two or more partners) and only a little more than one fifth have ever restricted themselves "primarily" to one partner for more than a year.[30]

Former Kinsey associate William Simon, now at the University of Chicago, has described a survey indicating the transitory character of most male homosexual experience: "About half reported that 60 percent or more of their sexual partners were persons with whom they had sex only one time. Between 10 and 20 percent reported that they often picked up their partners in public toilets. An even larger proportion reported similar contacts in other public or semi-public locations. Between a quarter and a third reported being robbed by a sexual partner."[31] Since public pickups of unknown persons offer the largest danger of arrest, venereal disease, and physical attack, the persistent homosexual male preference for this activity suggests the promiscuous character of the male sex drive undisciplined by monogamous women.

Homosexuals do not appear to be strikingly more neurotic in other ways than straight singles. At the time of the Kinsey survey only 7.6 percent were consulting psychiatrists, a little less than other singles and substantially less than divorced men.[32] The chief complaints of homosexual men seem to be what the survey classed as "psychosomatic symptoms." Eighty-five percent were alleged to be frequently afflicted by headaches and by upset stomachs, and 65 percent were bothered by trembling hands—percentages more than triple those for normal single men.[33]

The over-all impact of homosexuals on the statistics remains obscure, however. Some fragmentary reports indicate that homosexuals earn more money, commit less crime, and live longer than heterosexual singles. Other reports suggest that they are more prone to commit suicide. It is likely, therefore, that gays will slightly improve some of the single male statistics (income, crime, expressed happiness) and worsen others (venereal disease, suicide, and psychosomatic symptoms).[34] But there is little solid data available.

In any case, homosexuals are usually single men and they suffer from the same problems of rootlessness and impulsiveness that characterize single male life in general. In fact, their sex lives seem to be almost a caricature of normal single male compulsiveness and promiscuity. (Similarly, lesbians, in their tendency toward long-term relationships, resemble normal females far more than they resemble male homosexuals. The homosexual community thus provides further evidence to support the thesis that long-term relationships are chiefly evoked by the female role in human sexuality.) What statistics are available suggest that male homosexuals are far more like male singles than like female homosexuals or any other group in the population.

Needless to say, all such surveys are fallible. Studies based on vague criteria of mental health and happiness lack any final authority. The question of whether single or married women are in better shape remains very much at issue. Single women get sick and are more often institutionalized, but married women seem to show many more neurotic symptoms. The surveys are unanimous on one point, however: that single men of all sexual orientations are in drastically worse shape than married men or married and single women. They compound their economic weaknesses with severe physical and psychological problems that get worse as they grow older unmarried.

These conclusions are heavily supported by data from institutions, both for chronic disease and for mental illness. These statistics, indicating conditions serious enough for hospitalization, are beyond dispute. Single men are proportionately ten times more likely than married men to be put in hospitals for chronic diseases.[35] But the really striking figures come from mental hospitals. Bachelors are twenty-two times more likely than married men to be committed for mental disease.[36] (Single women, incidentally, are about ten times more likely to be committed than married women.) Of the 244,770 men in mental institutions, only 38 percent have ever been married and almost half of *them* have been widowed or divorced.[37]

These figures are not surprising. One would not expect a high proportion of psychotics—even potential psychotics—to be marriageable, even if the psychosis develops late in life. Still, about two thirds of all *female* inmates have been married.[38]

The institutionalized men assume significance chiefly as part of the larger pattern of social distresses surrounding single males. If you are going to write about "madness," bachelors seem to be your quarry. If you want to write about "discrimination" and "waste of human resources," single men seem to serve your purposes about as well as most other groups.

As far as the society is concerned, however, the main problem of single men is not mental or physical illness, or related afflictions like alcoholism and loneliness. It is not discrimination or poverty. It is not that thriving old specialty of single men and their intimates: venereal disease. Single men have another way of getting the rest of the society, however reluctantly and unconsciously, to take part in their problems. That way is crime.

Much verbiage has been shed on the issue of whether crime is chiefly a function of mental disease—psychological "madness"—or whether it is chiefly an effect of social conditions, an expression of "madness" against "an unjust society." Such analyses usually circle round and round the central fact about crime. They treat crime as if it were committed by "persons" or "human beings"—those neutral sociological units adopted in order to avoid offending anyone. These units are routinely compared in terms of age, housing, education, income, and geographical location. Then with all due apologies to Roy Wilkins and Senator Brooke, condemnation of unreported "crime in the suites," invocations of Watergate, lamentations on slavery and prejudice, denunciation of the Vietnam War, it is observed that about half of all crime is committed by and against blacks.

Nonetheless, the central facts about crime are not racial. They are sexual. Groups of sociologists venturing into urban streets after their seminars on violence in America do not rush to their taxis fearing attack by marauding bands of feminists, covens of single women, or angry packs of welfare mothers. Despite all the movies of the *Bonnie and Clyde* genre, and the exploits of the Symbionese Liberation Army, one need have little fear of any group that so much as contains women—or, if the truth be known, of any group that contains men who are married to women. Crime, like poverty, correlates better with sex and singleness than it does with race.

Some 3 percent of criminals are women; only 33 percent are married men. Although single men number 13 percent of the population over age fourteen, they comprise 60 percent of the criminals and commit about 90 percent of major and violent crimes. If one includes divorced men among the singles, the percentage of single criminals rises toward 75 percent,[39] but the statistics are unclear on what proportion were divorced *after* they were convicted of crime.

Of course, a large number of all crimes—and a still larger proportion of violent crimes—are committed by single men under twenty-five. In fact, about 55 percent of all single male prisoners in 1970 were between the ages of fourteen and twenty-four. But even in the age group between twenty and twenty-four, single men were proportionately almost two and a half times more likely than married men to be imprisoned; and in the twenty-five to sixty-five group, single men were proportionately over seven times more likely to be incarcerated than married men.[40]

So violence and crime join with "madness," mental illness, mild neurosis, depression, addiction, venereal disease, chronic disability, psychiatric treatment, loneliness, insomnia, institutionalization, poverty, "discrimination," unemployment, and nightmares as part of the specialized culture of single men in America. The climax of the grim story, however, is death. It is not surprising that the single male mortality rate, also, is the highest of all.

2

The Death of a Single Man

> When we have no other object than ourselves we cannot avoid the thought that our efforts will finally end in nothingness . . . . The bond attaching man to life relaxes because that attaching him to society is itself slack . . . .
>
> —EMILE DURKHEIM (*discussing the disproportionate number of suicides by single men in 19th-century France, Sweden and Italy*), Suicide

We live together, it is said, but we die alone. All too often, single men have lives as solitary as their deaths. But the one I am going to tell you about did not die alone.

The mortality rate among my boyhood friends is low. Of the five boys with whom I was closest as I grew up in the Berkshires, only one is dead now, as far as I know. The rest are all married—at last report, happily—and have moved beyond the ken of these ruminations. P.J. was the one who died.

I remember him as a tough, crew-cut teenager, with well-muscled arms, shirtsleeves ripped off at the shoulder, and a broad smile, slightly askew, happily responsive to the absurdities of his world. One learned not to talk much about his parents, who were divorced, I gathered, and a problem for him. We used to roughhouse and play hockey or football together, and later go on wild drives in his car. Then I would occasionally stay over at his house, a large farmhouse in our secluded Berkshire valley, with pastures dappled with cattle, and dark evergreen hills looming up all around. We would talk late into the night about sports and girls and when we would get laid, and what manly honors his cousins had won in various military ventures.

We also followed the same circuit of summer and vacation parties. P.J. used to spend them drinking beer and talking loudly, charmingly, obscenely, hilariously about his problems with the various prep schools, automobiles, girls, and sports events in his life. I used to spend them listening to P.J., until he got too drunk to include any intelligible nouns and verbs among his spatter of sexual expletives. I would then turn to my pursuit of the Kays and Charlottes, Mikalas and Debbies, Kates and Peppers who inhabited my dreams—in the hopes of exhausting their defenses by the end of the evening. P.J., though, drunk or sober, seemed to do better than I did. At least he said he did, said he got all kinds of "tail." Maybe he did, at that.

I went off to college and P.J. joined the Marines, but he was not exactly a casualty of the war. He entered too early for Vietnam. That was probably too bad, since combat might well have saved his life. As it was, he was a splendid Marine, a frogman so adept that he was assigned to a special unit chiefly used for exhibitions. When I skulked home after flunking out of college, I met P.J. on leave, and there seemed no doubt at the time that he had made a better choice than I had. Bronzed, fit, confident, charming as ever, he seemed a winner. I remember marveling at how he had raised the use of the word "fuck" to a high art, inflecting it, conjugating it, swaggering it. He added enough suffixes and prefixes to outfit a Greek verb—communicating a sense of being at home, a man, in his language in a way I had never achieved. P.J. persuaded me to join the Marines and within my first five minutes at Parris Island I was to learn that his was not a unique talent. But at the time, like his uniform, his stripes, his medals, it seemed somehow a badge of manhood, and like most teenagers, I was busy trying to figure out just what manhood was. I was looking for the test, the ritual, that would certify me and allow me to get on with my life. P.J. seemed to have found a way.

He stayed in the service for some years after that, gathering more stripes and honors. I sometimes saw him when he came home on leave, though, and he was tired of the endless round of maneuvers and exhibitions to which he was assigned in the South. He wanted to get to Vietnam, where the action was beginning. I suppose he needed a new, bloodier rite of passage. I do not mean that he needed specifically to kill. I do not believe men need to kill. But in the Marines, the man who has not faced combat is always in a caste below the men who have. It is the ultimate test and P.J. wanted to meet it.

I never saw him again after that. I know he was not sent to Vietnam. Instead he languished first in Korea and then in various U.S. bases. Here he was denied the chance to fight external enemies, and denied as well—Marines will tell you— the chance to find love. Most men join the Marines at least in part as a virility rite, with women assumed as a reward, and P.J. certainly did have such a vision. But they early discover that there are no women to be had. Certainly few "nice girls" are ready to fall before the urgencies of a man with just two weeks to make it before his leave is up—even if he wears his medals and dress blues twenty-four hours a day and buys a wig to cover his crewcut. He is treated as if he has some rare and refractory form of V.D. He soon concludes that however pretty it is, his body is worthless to most women. It is desired chiefly by homosexuals. A woman's body, on the other hand, he finds is anything but worthless. He has to pay to see it, pay for every inch he touches of it, pay two weeks of wages to fuck it, and often pay afterward to get rid of resulting diseases. He learns to fear and distrust women.

So one imagines P.J. stranded in North Carolina, without much sex or challenge, hunched over a bar, finding the next beer too much like the last, the next day too much like the one before—his manhood, so arduously won, slipping away just when he needs it most. For he discovers that there are enemies more menacing and elusive than the Vietcong and they are bringing the war home to him.

All this is speculation. It is not speculation, however, that P.J. became a warrior with no one to fight but himself. And nowhere in his cartridge belt, his paratroopers' handbook, or his panoply of grenades, rifles, and practical skills was there any good defense. His great physical courage, his taut armature of sinew—even his awesome capacity to drink —would get him nowhere against the demons that, perhaps pursuing him ever since his childhood, finally caught up with him in a dreary Southern motel room one warm spring day in 1969.

Single men are not in general very good at life. Often they know little about the most important parts of it. But they are sometimes fiercely ingenious at death. If you want a troop of killers, the military has learned, it is best to stick with the singles. Whether you are a Maoist who wants Red Guards to terrorize the land, an Indonesian general intent on massacring Chinese, a Ugandan out to banish Indians, a Nazi recruiting storm troopers, or an American officer looking for men equal to a Mylai, you stay away from the securely married. You want your lieutenants callow and womanless.

Throughout human history, war and killing have been significant ways of disposing of single men. Even in troops of baboons the lowest-ranking males are the ones in the vanguard or on the flanks, the ones who face the leopard or the lion. Throughout human evolution, single men have been the first to kill and be killed. Women and children and dominant males are obviously more important to the survival of a group. And the young men have accepted this order of life, or it could not have prevailed. They have known in their bones and hearts that ultimately they are *dispensable*. They are the ones to leap on the grenade or charge the enemy bunker.

Single men, therefore, join the ability to kill with a knowledge of their own expendability. It is a terrible combination when they lose their sense of ever reaching the dominant class; when they despair of being wanted by women and needed by society; when they feel they cannot meet the test and make it as men; when, indeed, they cannot even find the testing ground. Then their talent for death can be turned against themselves. And they are brilliant at it.

Single male suicides do not mess around: no half-hacked wrists, or semi-signaled sleeping pills, or window ledge posturings. They *do* it, coolly, fiercely, efficiently. They do it four times as often as young married men, five times as often as married women, four times as often as single women.[1] One of them I know about—a charming, intelligent young man— was interrupted by the milkman as he tried to gas himself. The boy conversed calmly for twenty minutes, disarming all suspicion, and then proceeded to finish the job. Another acquaintance, an extraordinary boy, escaped from a mental hospital and used his expert mechanical and tactical knowledge to build a perfect gallows in a darkened cellar, where he would be discovered by his mother when she turned on the lights to do the laundry. And then there was P.J.

The story of P.J.'s death reached me later by the grapevine. The people who saw it did not want to talk about it and I was not informed of the funeral. I understand he invited his two long-separated parents to attend some Marine Corps ceremony. They were told to meet him at a motel near the base. They came down, but the ceremony they saw was not what they expected. Joined in the motel room, assembled as witnesses, they found P.J. with a .45. It was, one gathered, to be a suicide with a message, no less intelligible for being unwritten. He shot himself in the head as they watched.

I suppose P.J.'s death can be dismissed as a case of special psychopathy. I admit he had a special vulnerability; most sick people do. But he managed to send important messages to me.

Suicide is increasingly the way young men die. Sadly, it it is not only P.J. who had encountered a blight on his passage to manhood in America—a blight as deadly as our wars. If we are to overcome it, we must address ourselves to the special problems of young men. We must try to understand why they are vulnerable and violent; how their bodies and minds are in such imperious flux; why nearly every society known to anthropologists provides special rituals of initiation and passage for its boys; how this society is blurring or destroying all the lines of male demarkation, replacing the usual series of tests and rituals with a no man's land—a sexually neutral arena where one becomes an "adult human being" by "doing one's own thing." And finally we might come to understand why this country, more than any other in the world, is preoccupied with the anarchic violence of its youth.

Suicide is not restricted to young men, however. In fact, after the perilous early twenties, the older a man gets without marrying the more likely he is to kill himself. In addition, there are many forms of suicide that are listed under other names. Single men have about double the mortality rate of married men and three times the mortality rate of single women from all causes: from automobile accidents and other mishaps, as well as from the whole range of conventional diseases.[2] Most of the illnesses do not become evident until after age forty-five. Many of them, it is safe to say, represent various forms of disguised or unconscious suicide.

One of the chief ultimate causes of death throughout the animal kingdom is a collapse of the will to live. Healthy animals of many kinds die in captivity. Dominant baboons and other animals often die of "natural" causes shortly after losing their positions to younger rivals. Primitive tribes suffer high death rates when economic change or technology destroys their culture. American politicians often die shortly after defeat ends their careers.

In analyzing the high death rates of single men, sociologists normally focus on the bachelors' lack of the kind of "personal maintenance" married men enjoy from their wives. Feminists talk of the failure of sexist society to teach male children how to cook and take care of themselves.

But this notion completely misses the point. Single men are perfectly capable of taking care of their physical needs when they want to. Most of them can cook, sew, clean up, and perform other "maintenance" tasks. The problem is the will, not the way. Like P.J., they don't care enough.

The maintenance explanations are inadequate to explain the all-encompassing reach of single male afflictions. Is it not more likely, for example, that if heart attacks were banished, one would merely find many of these men dying in other ways—or swelling the ranks of the mentally ill? Altogether the pattern of mortality among single men is so various and inexorable that it suggests an organic source: a failure of the will to live, a disconnection from the life force itself as it arises in society.

Men need women—far more than women need men—for their very survival. Men need a biological and sexual tie of the sort uniquely provided by marriage and children. Otherwise they are relegated to the optional fringes of life; and, like single warriors, they know they are dispensable. The struggle for marriage and family is a struggle for life itself.

The problem is that men do not necessarily know this. Like P.J., they continue to pursue an obsolesent manhood of the hunting party. They become increasingly alienated from the patterns of family life, which offer the only widely available way to work out a full manhood of seventy years.

Perhaps the most dramatic evidence of the importance of the marriage tie to men is the impact of its rupture by divorce or widowhood. Contrary to the usual images of the helpless and abandoned wife, the statistics show far greater evidence of helpless and traumatized husbands. The wages of divorce for men, to an astonishing degree, turn out to be death. It is men, surprisingly enough, who seem to be the divorce losers.

The Divorce Losers

It is necessary to renounce a freedom that does not exist and
to recognize a dependency of which we are not conscious.
—LEO TOLSTOY

In a secular society, children are the last sacred objects.
—JOSEPH EPSTEIN

In the part of the country where I live, there are considerable numbers of middle-aged divorced men. Many of them
have money, often by inheritance. Few of them work in any
discernably productive way. They purport to be writing a
novel or a screenplay, or to be inventing a new kind of automobile engine, or to be resolving some conundrum of twelve-
tone music. They tend to drink too much. Although they have
freedom, money, and often sex, many of them seem to be
destroying themselves, slowly but inexorably.

One of them, Paul Ailey, wrote a novel fifteen years ago
that was highly praised by both Edmund Wilson and Jack
Kerouac. Largely autobiographical, it afforded him his life's
most delicious moments when he watched himself being played
in the movie by Paul Newman. Ailey was the only person who
had ever previously noticed any resemblance. Most people,
Ailey thought, were misled because he was so much taller than
Paul Newman.

Ailey's novel, *The War Home,* made him an instant contender in The Big Novel Sweepstakes. Norman Mailer noticed. There was wide speculation about Ailey's second novel, supposedly in progress. Expectations lowered slightly when three years later a part of it was published in *Partisan Review.* The excerpt was a short story essentially repeating a celebrated sex scene from *The War Home.* It had seemed startling and original when it appeared in the novel, but there had been a lot of shocking pink prose published in the interim.

Twelve years later, no one is waiting any longer for Ailey to write. *The War Home* is difficult to purchase even in paperback. Although Mailer now lives only four miles away from Ailey's house, Mailer no longer notices.

Rather than finish another novel, Ailey seven years ago divorced his wife, a smart and lovely Englishwoman who had borne him two children, in order to pursue Liz Azar, a young movie starlet. Both he and Hollywood have long ago forgotten Liz. She moved to Ibiza, where she once occasionally consorted with Clifford Irving, and now consorts with a former admirer of Clifford Irving.

Ailey's wife, however, startled the world, and Ailey, by publishing a best-selling novel. Ailey felt the book jacket told it all: A young woman in a long dress, with blond hair billowing behind, was shown running in glamorous terror from a large Gothic house. A tree bent starkly in the wind under a wuthering sky. "Drivel," said Ailey. "Three hundred thousand," said Bantam Books. "Seven hundred thousand," said Warner Brothers. Her second novel is well under way and is eagerly awaited by millions of dollars.

Ailey is wearing a filmy light-green shirt of Indian origin, a small cowhide vest, tight blue jeans, and golden Puma track shoes. His sparse strands of hair almost cover his ears. He is sitting on the grass outside a white clapboard house, listening to the primal shrieks of his lover, Teresa, faintly audible from a closed upstairs room.

Ailey met Teresa two years ago at a jazz concert given by Charles Mingus at the Leonx Music Barn. They have lived together ever since. For his capture of Teresa, Ailey is highly envied by much of the Williams College class of 1972 and by assorted Yale and Harvard students, all of whom fell in love with her the first time they saw her lying on the wide lawns of Bennington. No one slept with her, however, before the night of the concert, when she was proud to sleep with the author of *The War Home*.

Since then Teresa has sampled most of the psychiatrists of Berkshire County, but the one she likes best is Dr. Fox, the primal therapist whom she is seeing now. Normally she strips to her underwear, lies back on the couch, and breathes deeply until she feels her whole body relax, and her thighs "stream" with tingling flows of what she assumes is Reichian "orgone" energy. She particularly enjoys it when Dr. Fox pushes down hard on her ribs to make her breathe more deeply. After about fifteen minutes of breathing, she is allowed to kick and beat at the bed. The relief is overwhelming. Then in the end she is allowed to scream. She shrieks and screams ecstatically for several minutes and the session ends. Ailey knows that he can expect her to come out, her face glowing with erotic promise, about ten minutes after the screaming starts.

Today she does not come out. Ailey wonders what is going on, but he does not much worry, since he is immersed in the transcripts of Watergate in *The New York Times*.

Dr. Fox, however, is inside making love to Teresa and wondering whether he should leave his wife. Teresa is overwhelmingly the most beautiful woman he has ever had, and Teresa finds Dr. Fox the most warm and reassuring lover she has ever had. She likes his fatherly calmness after Ailey's exertions, performed over her like hurried pushups. In fact, she has noticed that Ailey's face looks almost the same during his morning exercises as during his nocturnal ones, except that during his calisthenics he does not spray her face with

his whiskey breath. By contrast, Dr. Fox looks so fathom-
lessly wise and sure. She wonders how she can tell Ailey that
she plans to leave him . . .

Elliot Larkin sat on a bench in Central Park, losing an
argument with his son, Ellie, on the divinity of a black
preacher named Divine Daddy Jefferson.

This was a great strain to him. Elliot was an atheist,
whose toleration of religion reached only to the most hard-
nosed edges of agnosticism. In earlier years, he had delighted
to hear his son, at the age of five, doggedly resist the teachings
of his mother, Susan, on the existence of God.

With all the precocious authority of young Jesus in the
temple, Ellie would reject the notion of heaven. "When you
die, you die, that's all. You just rot in the ground." His mother
would try to persuade Ellie of a distinction between body and
soul. "You are not just your body. There is something else.
How can your thoughts, your memories, your real self rot?"

Ellie would look briefly solemn and perplexed. Then he
would sweep such distinctions aside. "My mind will rot, too,"
he would say, "so I can't think any more when I'm dead."
Elliot remembered grinning triumphantly behind his news-
paper, while his wife went on, with more futile arguments.
Susan could not shake the beliefs that Elliot had given his
son during those years of bedtime catechisms and walks in the
park. Ellie had been his father's boy.

But there had been a divorce and Ellie now was moving
away from him. Elliot had arranged to get his son every Sunday morning, just when Susan was going to church. During
the week, however, Ellie belonged to Susan, or worse. Now
it appeared that Ellie belonged to a black housekeeper, named
"Beatifying Grace," whom Susan had hired to free her for
her new career as an editor at Rancour House. Ellie was now
using his precocious intelligence to defend an itinerant preacher
who, like Father Divine before him, claimed to be God.

"Why do you believe in Divine Daddy?" Elliot asked his son. "What can *he* do for you?"

"He stops the police," Ellie said, with the same nod of assurance that he had previously used so endearingly against his mother. It was one of Elliot's own most distinctive mannerisms.

"What do you mean, stops the police?" Elliot asked with irritation.

"He stops the police from coming when I'm bad," Ellie said. "When I kick Grace, she calls the police on the phone. But I kneel at the window and pray to Divine Daddy and the police don't stop. They drive right by the house. Sometimes they slow down. But they don't stop if I pray to Divine Daddy."

"Let me get that straight. You mean to tell me that Grace pretends to telephone the police, and then . . ."

"She *does* call the police. I *see* her."

"All right, she calls the police and then tells you that you can stop them from coming by praying . . . praying to Big Daddy, or whoever?"

"Yes, and he stops them."

"Dammit," Elliot said, "they drive by the house all the time anyway. They *never* stop."

"Divine Daddy stops them from stopping. Grace calls for them to take me to jail. But they go right by if I pray to Divine Daddy. They even turn off their sirens."

"Goddammit, I'll sue that bitch," Elliot said.

"She's *not* a bitch," Ellie said. "She's an angel of Divine Daddy."

Elliot exploded: "Your real daddy is going to beat your ass if you talk like that any more."

Ellie's face twisted and he began to cry.

Elliot reached out to him. "I'm sorry I said that. I'm sorry, Ellie." But Ellie wrenched himself away.

"I'll tell you what," Elliot suggested, "let's go to the zoo and get a popsickle. Would you like a popsickle?"

"I don't want a popsickle. I want to go home," Ellie said.

"No, you can't go home until six o'clock," Elliot said.

"Why?" Ellie asked.

Because the judge said so, because I and my lawyer fought for nearly three months to prevent Susan from taking you away to San Francisco, because I drove 130 miles down from Massachusetts to see you, because I agreed to a fifteen-dollar-a-week increase in alimony in order to make sure I could have you every week, because your mother is making you into a weak, neurotic kid who prays to some black charlatan, because . . .

"Because I love you, Ellie, and I need to have you with me," Elliot said.

"I want to go back to Mommy," Ellie answered flatly.

Elliot remained silent.

Ellie continued to cry.

"Would you like to go to a movie?" Elliot suggested forlornly. The year before he had resolved never to waste his precious hours with Ellie sitting in a theater.

But at the mention of movies Ellie's face instantly brightened. "Yes, yes. A movie."

So Elliot found himself taking his son to a Clint Eastwood Western. Elliot believed that violent movies were the real pornography in America, but if it took Clint Eastwood to stop his son from crying, Clint Eastwood it had to be.

Elliot, however, decided he would not go through these Sunday agonies any longer. Susan had won, at least for now. When he took his son home and watched him run into his mother's welcoming arms at the door, into her comforting breasts, Elliot had to turn away to conceal his tears, suppress his desire to follow.

As he walked back to the street, he felt as if he had suffered some grave internal amputation, as if some life growing within him had been aborted. He entered a bar on the corner. Three hours later he was still there, but the anesthetic whiskey had not yet deadened the pain.

A common image of divorce finds the woman broke and abandoned, trapped by complaining children, and grasping at alcohol and tranquilizers—if not the delivery boy—to postpone an impending breakdown. The man, meanwhile, wretch that he is, becomes a sexual reveler who has his own way with women.

A more reasonable view is that in most divorces, particularly the 60 percent involving children, everyone loses. The woman is often left with the responsibility for both providing and caring for her children, although her most employable— and marriageable—years are over. The man loses his children, except for brief and complicated visits. And the children lose a stable home, with an available father. Thus they have no clear model of successful marriage and their ability to start or sustain a home in the future is impaired.

Most of these notions are plausible and true, particularly the idea of damage to children. But there is much evidence also to support another view: that the chief victim of most divorces is the man. The woman tends to suffer most during the separation, when the man diverts himself with dreams of bachelor freedom. If she is over forty, she has a much smaller chance for remarriage. But in terms of mental and physical disease and life expectancy, divorce damages the man far more than the woman.

A Jewish proverb holds that the single woman is a tragedy, while the single man is a clown. And comic—or tragic-comic—figures persist today among the men who lose at divorce. Whether cuckolded, or seduced by a dream of youth, the divorced man often loses his dignity. Like some divorced women, a number of the men obsess themselves with plans of vengeance against their former spouses. Others quixotically tilt at teenagers or posture hopelessly at other men's wives.

The emotional strains on divorced men with children reduce both their ability to earn money and their willingness to part with it. As a result, the most extreme cases end up in jail.

The New York Times tells of Sol Greenberg of Brooklyn. At the time of his divorce he was making a lot of money in the camera business. With the advice of a lawyer, who was the uncle of his wife, he agreed to pay 75 dollars a week in child support. While one might wonder about a man who gets his wife's uncle for a lawyer in a divorce proceeding, it seemed a good way to save money at the time; and, anyway, everybody was buying cameras.

The camera store went out of business, however, and he was left with this bill of 75 dollars a week. It soon added up to 3,000 dollars. Sol could not or would not pay and was dispatched to jail for six months by the judge, for civil contempt. In such cases there is no jury trial and no bail. You pay or you serve your time.[1]

Or else you leave the country. This was the solution chosen by a former movie stuntman, call him Errol, who was an expert fencer. He was big time in the days when historical dramas, full of acrobatic swordplay, were the rage. So when he was divorced he made a big-time commitment to his wife and three children.

Distributors, however, began to take the line that "we don't want any more pictures where they write with feathers." This posed a problem for Errol. In the movies, swords and quill pens go together like arrows and feathers. So our stuntman's income began to decline. He could no longer manage his alimony payments. Ultimately he spent several months in the same Brooklyn jail and then left the country. He is said to have taken up a new career as a cat thief on the Riviera. A less romantic and more believable story has him as one of the Riviera's many alcoholic con men. He no longer ever sees his children.

Divorced men suffer most of the financial difficulties of

single men, and incur new responsibilities. In part because of their emotional turmoil, divorced men make about 20 percent less than married men of the same age, while singles earn 40 percent less.[2]

Even if he remains successful, however, the divorced man is often in a far worse financial position than either his single or married contemporaries. The divorced man usually has two households to support. This can be hard, particularly if he decides to try to marry again or conduct an active social life.

These financial problems are aggravated by bitterness toward the former wives and by a wide range of mental distresses, from mild depression to real psychosis.

Divorced men lead the league in mental illness. Phyllis Chesler's figures indicate that they are two times more likely than single men—and five times more likely than married men —to become psychiatric outpatients. They are 10 percent more likely to seek psychiatric help than divorced and separated women.[3]

According to the figures presented by Jessie Bernard— which, like all data on vague concepts like happiness, are useful chiefly as corroborating evidence—divorced men are two times more likely even than single men to consider themselves unhappy. Divorced men are four times more likely than married men to profess unhappiness. And they are 50 percent more prone to unhappiness than divorced women.[4]

A description of the membership in Parents Without Partners—a rapidly growing nationwide group with some 100,000 members trying to escape the singles life—confirms this picture. In his popular survey of singles organizations, psychologist Andrew du Brin reported that "female PWP members tend to be healthier than their male counterparts. Most of the male members, it appears, have some serious problems about women, divorce, or responsibility. Some members spend all their evenings either in bars or at PWP meetings."[5]

Bars and PWP meetings are among the nicer haunts of divorced men. ·They also can be found in disproportionate numbers in mental hospitals and prisons. Although the census figures do not indicate adequately whether a divorce was an effect of the institutionalization or a cause of it, the statistics are useful in conjunction with other data. They indicate to some extent the comparative condition of divorced men and women. In asylums as in prisons—in fact, wherever people are locked up—one finds vastly more men than women who have been divorced.

There were 1,344,597 divorced men in 1970 between the ages of twenty-five and sixty-five. Of these, about 70,000, or about 5 percent, were in prisons or mental institutions, compared to 1.5 percent of divorced women and 7 percent of single men in the same age group.[6] In this age group, divorced men outnumber divorced women in mental hospitals by 25 percent, in all institutions and hospitals, excluding prisons, by 21 percent, and in prisons by 95 percent.[7]

It is in statistics of disease and mortality, however, that the plight of divorced men emerges most strikingly. According to recently corrected figures from the National Bureau of Health Statistics, divorced men between the ages of thirty-five and sixty-four have a mortality rate three and a third times as high as divorced women and two and one half times as high as married men. Divorced men die at a rate one third higher even than single men. The figures for widowed men are only slightly lower than for divorced men.[8]

They die of all causes, but, like single men, divorced men specialize in accidents and suicides. Divorced men are four times as likely as married men and three and a half times as likely as divorced women to commit suicide. They are about four times as likely as either married men or divorced women to die in automobile accidents, often a disguise for suicide. Like single men, they are six times more likely than married men and some twenty times more likely than divorced women to die of "accidental falls." They are eight times more likely than married men and four times more likely than divorced women to die in an accidental fire or explosion. Murder claims eight divorced men for every married one and three divorced men for every divorced woman. And, in the realm of more conventional mortality, divorced men are twice as likely as married men and six times as likely as divorced women to die of heart disease.[9]

Recent figures from Canada verify the pattern, for both the single and the divorced. The widowed and divorced of every age group, from twenty-five on, have death rates approximately three times higher than married men or divorced women. Even between the ages of twenty-five and forty-four, men who have lost their wives die about three times more often than married men or divorced women. The Canadian figures also indicate the degree that divorced men, trying to drown their sorrows in alcohol, end up drowning themselves in alcoholism. They die five times as often from cirrhosis of the liver as married men and more than three times as often as divorced women.[10]

Once again, as in the case of single men, we find that men need women far more than women need men. When a man, accepting an honor at the company banquet—or prefacing a book—gives much of the credit to his wife, he is not merely following a ritual. He is stating a practical fact. In overwhelming likelihood, he would not have succeeded—and possibly not even survived—if he had been single or divorced.

But no case is ever proved in the social sciences. Statistics are treacherous. One must take care to avoid the seductive fallacy of *post hoc ergo propter hoc*—of ascribing causation to what may be mere sequence. Perhaps, as skeptics would point out, all these weaknesses of the single and divorced are the cause of their marital failures. The man with a criminal bent or a proneness for mental illness is admittedly a poor prospect for marriage and a good one for divorce. Perhaps the man who falls off cliffs, or crashes his automobile, or drinks to excess, or takes addictive drugs, or fools around with

guns, or inclines to suicide, or becomes depressed and unhappy and neurotic—*even late in life*—perhaps these men
also, in one way or another, selected themselves out for successful marriage.

It is possible to explain by the process of marital selection all associations of divorced and single men with mortality,
insanity, and criminality—and the associations of married
men with longevity, success, and equanimity. It is possible to
contend that these statistical relationships have little to do
with the comparative healthiness of single and married life
or the deep psychological need of men for women. But these
explanations create more problems than they solve. The idea
that most of the singles had been inherently unmarriageable
and the divorced had been unstable fails to explain the same
pattern of afflictions among widowers. It fails to explain the
absence of comparable patterns among single and divorced
women. And the marital selection theory fails to explain the
mechanism whereby many of the symptoms that supposedly
prevent marriage do not appear until after many years of
singleness. In addition, the impact of marriage on character
is not merely a statistical notion. One does not have to look
far to find examples of buccaneer singles transformed by marriage or to find examples of once stable men plunged into
depression and drink by widowhood or divorce.

Other skeptics ascribe all the problems of divorced men
to the removal of personal maintenance. But this theory fails
to explain why the pattern affects the rich, who can have
maids, as well as the poor, who cannot, and affects the young
and the old, from all parts of the country and from all industrial societies where statistics are available. There is little
evidence even for the view that a lack of sex is the problem
of the divorced. The recent *Playboy* study *Sex in the Seventies*
indicates that divorced men have sex as much as married
ones.[11]

There is no question, however, that the lack of personal
maintenance—and the fewer marriages among the sick and

criminal—have some impact on the data. But there are better theories, which have to do with the profound biological need of men for families and the crucial role of love and marriage in building a civilized society. One discovers, in fact, that it is nearly impossible to explain how a society works without an understanding of the role of responsible love.

In the elaborate studies by John Bowlby on attachment and loss in small children in all human societies,[12] in recent evidence that lack of "social involvement" is a key to mental illness, and in the endless annals of the literature of isolation, everywhere we discover that the finding and losing of love are central to human experience. It should not be surprising that divorce is a deadly event for men. Men are usually the most active partners in the finding of love, and they are most likely to lose everything, even the children, when love is lost.

The plight of a man, divorced and loveless, was poignantly described by John Cheever in an allegorical but somehow thoroughly believable short story. Called *The Swimmer,* it was later made into an interesting but inadequate movie by Frank Perry. In the story, the man resolves to swim his way home through all the pools in Westchester County, one after another, "portaging" between them, until he gets back to his house. He sets out, full of enthusiasm, thrashing energetically through the water, like a divorced man reveling in his first affairs after marriage. But after a while he tires, and the water is no longer refreshing, and the women he meets along the way no longer replenish him, and he becomes ever more erratic and compulsive, until at last he arrives at the door of his house, now empty and in ruin. He is left in the rain, near naked, with nowhere at all to go.

This is, of course, a melodramatic picture of what happens to a divorced man, who becomes in a sense biologically stranded. But melodramatic or not, it bears a powerful message at a time when it is assumed that divorces can continue at their current rate indefinitely without grave damage to the society.

4

Lennie and Frank at "Love Unlimited"

Gatsby believed in the green light, the orgiastic future that year by year recedes before us. It eluded us then, but that's no matter—tomorrow we will run faster, stretch out our arms farther. . . . And one fine morning—

So we beat on, boats against the current, borne back ceaselessly into the past.

—F. Scott Fitzgerald

Two Harvard professors in their late thirties, one single, the other just divorced, arrived in the palmy air of Los Angeles last year from a dank and frigid winter in Boston. It was partly the martinis they had had on the flight. But probably it was more the sudden bath of California warmth—pouring into them at the airport like an uncanny early fever of spring along the Charles (on a day, to be sure, when the breezes are mingled with fumes from Memorial Drive).

Perhaps, too, it was the smarmy air of America in the early 1970s—a sense that things were going sour—joined with a faith in the Green Light at the end of the tunnel, when all systems would be go for the orgiastic future. Whatever it was, their intention of taking the bus out to U.C.L.A. for a conference on The Crisis in Civil Liberties did not survive their passage through the airport. They decided to celebrate Lennie's divorce by going out on the town and finding themselves some girls.

In the taxicab, Lennie asked the driver where "it was at" on a Friday night in L.A. A young light-skinned black with an Afro, he quickly appraised Lennie's longish blond hair and wire glasses and said a lot of the local people go to a place called The Stockyard.

"I've heard of it," Lennie said. "Jimmy Brown used to go there, didn't he?"

"Could be," the driver replied. "Like I said, it's the place to go."

The Stockyard turned out to be a big plush and plastic bar and steakhouse, full of loud music and young Californians. They came in all colors and a single creed, which seemed to the two visitors to be, like the very California breeze, full of sexual promise.

But Frank and Lennie never figured out the language. Frank focused modestly on the older women present, the ones possibly in their thirties. Most of them slipped away to the side as he accosted them, as if they were reversed magnets. Others turned breastily toward him with a note of irritation.

"This is an interesting place," he ventured to one.

"What?" she asked, her patience running out.

"This is an interesting place!" he repeated. The girl looked at him blankly and turned away, patience exhausted.

Now Frank, though pleasant and athletic looking, is acknowledged by his friends to be something of an acquired taste. He was at a disadvantage in The Stockyard, where few had read his treatise on *The Social Roots of McCarthyism*. Conversationally he is slow. His readiest wit, for example, is contained in a joke book, alphabetized by subject, that he carries around in his pocket and consults furtively at dinner parties. Frank's previous girl friends had been the result of prolonged pursuit, and his last lover, an abortive fiancée, had been a Boston University assistant professor in his own field. Admittedly Frank was a taste not easily acquired in a Los Angeles singles bar.

But Lennie is a different story. Although he comes from Portsmouth, New Hampshire, in Cambridge he is regarded as positively Californian. He often wears his shirts rakishly unbuttoned (two down from the top) to reveal a fuzzy swatch of chest, and he is reportedly the one who explained the Rolling Stones to Daniel Ellsberg during Ellsberg's sudden conversion to the counterculture. And even during his ten-year marriage, which had given him two young sons, Lennie had become one of the leading rakes of the Cambridge anti-war movement.

Lennie did do a little better at The Stockyard than Frank; the girls at least talked to him a bit. Still, when Frank came over and suggested that they go eat dinner, Lennie was glad to comply; and after dinner—a burned steak, on bread that stuck to the metal plate—he was glad to leave.

To find out what else was going on in the city, they bought a copy of the L.A. *Free Press,* a weekly that combines the idioms of *The Village Voice* and the New York *Daily News.* By that point they were half ready to settle for a movie, or a late consideration of Civil Liberties. But as Lennie thumbed through the paper, smiling at the heavy black headlines on witchcraft and Henry Kissinger, rape on the school buses, and the spiritual agony of Sonny and Cher—shaking his head at grave columns on astrology and Zen—he began to recover his sense of Eastern superiority and thus escape the pall of being rejected by Californian women who had never heard of Earl Warren. He assured himself that such a sheet could never be sold in Boston.

"It's amateur night all the way," he said, turning a page casually into a promised land of orgiastic sexual advertisements.

"What did you find?" Frank asked. "Let me see that."

Lennie was riveted.

"You know what, Frank," he said finally, solemnly. "You know what we are going to do tonight? Pardon me, but we're going to get laid."

The *Free Press* had blossomed into pages on pages of rhapsodic breasts and languorous lips and splayed thighs, advertising what seemed to be hundreds of "Houses of Pleasure," "Relaxation Pluses," "Venus Touches," "Roman Forums," "Tiger's Dens," "Pleasure Palaces," "Miracle Massages"— even a place called "Love Unlimited"—all offering Girls, Girls, Girls, in Private Rooms, promising Total Satisfaction! Complete Relaxation! Ultimate Pleasure!, even Ecstasy! All the things Lennie wanted that night. "But these are all just massage parlors," Frank said.

"Are you kidding!" Lennie laughed. "You know what massage parlors are. You expect 'em to call themselves whorehouses?" He slapped Frank on the back. "Cheer up—welcome to California!"

Despite demurrals from Frank, Lennie hailed a cab and they took it to a place called Max Roy's "Roman Palace of Pleasures." It advertised saunas and whirlpools, which Frank thought would go well after an orgy. Inside it was all plush carpets, soft couches, chandeliers, naked "Roman" statues. Dappling the wallpaper were amorphous shapes that a close look revealed to be Kama Sutra drawings. Through curtains, partly opened into the nether chambers, one could occasionally glimpse girls, girls, girls, lightly clad, in near darkness. And the vaguely Oriental Musak seemed to suggest that these girls would not offer mere girl-next-door sex but some more exotic way of aphrodisia.

A soft voice spoke from an alcove behind him. "I'm Sandra. Can I help you?"

Frank and Lennie started, then turned to face a tall woman with long blond hair and sumptuous breasts, who was draped in some happily inadequate toga. She smiled warmly at them. They did not speak. It was if they had been thrust suddenly, without a script, into one of the James Bond movies

—in which the hero is forever entering opulent rooms occupied only by absurdly clad and copious women, who are often holding guns. Sandra, as it turned out, did not need a gun.

"Would you like a massage?"

Lennie nodded.

"Are you together?"

"Yes," Frank said.

"No, separate," Lennie cut in.

"I understand. Your names, please?"

"Paul Andrews," Lennie said.

"First name is enough. I'll put Paul. Well, we have the Roman Special, which is a half an hour with one girl and a sauna. That's twenty-five dollars. We have the Roman Deluxe, which is a full hour with one girl with a sauna and whirlpool. That's thirty-five dollars. With a waterbed it's forty-five. And we specially recommend the Deluxe Roman Orgy, which is a full hour with two girls and a whirlpool bath and sauna. Of course, the Deluxe Orgy is in our special Cleopatra room with waterbed and mirrors on all sides."

"I'll take it," Lennie said.

"That costs seventy-five dollars."

"Okay," Lennie said.

"What was the second one?" Frank asked.

"That's our Roman Deluxe Massage. One girl for an hour, with a sauna and whirlpool. The waterbed is ten dollars extra."

"That's fine for me," he said.

"With or without the waterbed?"

Now warming to the evening, Frank replied "With."

"You'll like it," said Sandra confidently.

They were ushered into the next room and seated on soft couches to await their assigned girls. Cynthia came first to get Frank. As they walked away, Lennie called out, "Frank, don't ever tell me I never did anything for you . . ."

"You know what that was," Lennie said afterward. "That

was the sting! Damn! The girls didn't even take their clothes
off! What I particularly liked was that cool way she laid the
towel across my crotch at the beginning. I mean, she told me
to get undressed, and when I do, she acts like, don't I know
this is a *respectable* joint. We don't allow men with *those things*
in here! . . . Then they rub that lukewarm oil on you. Lukewarm, hell—in five minutes the stuff was frigid. I was actually shivering in there."

"Welcome to balmy California," Frank said.

"Shit," said Lennie.

Being Harvard professors, however, Lennie and Frank
were slow learners. And being liberal, they were unready to
condemn *all* massage parlors on the basis of one experience.
Lennie figured out that the problem was the place was too
posh. "A tourist trap," he said definitively. "Did you see they
had *Carte Blanche* and American Express?" The next time
they would go to a cheaper place, the kind of establishment
that would go out of business if it didn't deliver the goods. He
selected an ad for Tanya's; it seemed more shoddily desperate
than the others.

Thus it happened that a half hour later Lennie found
himself in a smoky, low-ceilinged room, stripped to his under-
pants, with a topless little Chinese girl—whose vocabulary
was limited to "You likey no?" and "Not on ploglam"—playing a game of pocket billiards. Lennie was allowed to dance
with her. He was allowed to watch television with her on a
waterbed. And he was allowed to play her a few games of
pocket billiards. But anything else, well, "Not on ploglam,
no." He played with great intensity. "Why not?" as he said
later, "it cost a dollar a ball, so to speak."

Frank, this time, was relatively pleased, for his girl had
allowed him to feel her breasts while they watched a Perry
Mason rerun from the waterbed. She had also given him an
address, where she assured him they could get laid.

"The girls at the Pussycat Corral do *everything*," she
said. Against all his experience, Frank imagined that any in-

formation costing a five-dollar tip must be valuable. He was assured, in any case, that they did not play pocket billiards at the Pussycat Corral.

The two professors hailed a cab and headed downtown. As they turned off Sunset Boulevard, Lennie spotted, on a grassy hill above the street, a large sign with a blinking purple light. LOVE UNLIMITED glowed in the California night. Lennie distinctly remembered the ad from the paper. It had offered girls who didn't "play around." "Our girls give you something to *come* for," it had said. Lennie was tempted to stop the cab there. It was just as well he didn't. If he had, we would have had the picture of the two professors laboring up the hill, entering breathlessly a small dark room with one purple light in the corner, paying 35 dollars to a large black man, then signing a card that denied any immoral intentions —"For your protection and ours," the man said with a wink —and all happily, happily, for the girls were a dream. There were two of them, with long blond hair, their mouths just open to curve the lips, the breasts softly shapely under dark tee-shirts—the kind of girls even Mick or Keith would joy to find in his bathtub on arriving in L.A. Yes, the professors would finally think their time had come in the promised land.

Then they would walk into the back room with their eyes on the perfect rears, young, smooth, subtly shifting under the soft jeans. The visitors would be aching with need—with all the long-gathered lust, accumulated year after year as each new crop of Radcliffe girls ripened before their eyes and de-parted untouched—but oh how deeply touching them.

No, it would have been too cruel for the two professors to go to LOVE UNLIMITED. A rare kind fate had saved them this time. For this is what would have happened.

After the girl had asked Lennie for her tip ahead of time ("Fifteen dollars is customary," she would have told him), and after he had eagerly paid, bringing the total to 50 dollars, she would have seated him briskly down on a couch and said, "I'm Carol, what would you like to talk about,

Lennie?" Lennie would have looked at her incredulously. Then he would have said, "I'd like to ball you." And she would have explained coolly that "Oh no, we don't do sex here. No immoral proposals, remember?" Slight pout. She would have looked a little disappointed in Lennie. Then a silver-lined smile: "But we can *talk* about sex, if you like. We have no limits on what we can talk about here."

Carol would have been as cheap as a psychiatrist, and far better looking, but still Lennie would not have understood. Even Frank would have approached the limits of his toleration. It is just as well they did not stop at LOVE UNLIMITED, particularly when just a mile away was the Pussycat Coral, where the girls did everything.

This establishment was on an intersection busy with "adult" bookstores and movie theaters far down Hollywood Boulevard toward downtown Los Angeles. A police car was parked on the corner and a young black was being pushed back on it to be frisked. A crowd gathered—curious, not angry, an assemblage of winos and whores and fat little men from the pornography stores. But it was enough to bring a sour taste of apprehension to Lennie and Frank as they approached the dingy little storefront with the flashing sign, Girls, Girls, Girls!

Loitering in front were two tough-looking blacks with a couple of white girls, one tall with fake silver hair, the other a brunette, with a bruised-looking face. Frank had had enough. "I'm not going," he said.

"Oh, come on," Lennie replied, "we've come too far to stop now."

"I'm not going," Frank said, "and that's that. If you insist, I'll wait in the drugstore on the corner."

"Suit yourself," Lennie said.

The group in front watched Lennie curiously as he pressed the button. He felt exposed on the street. Why didn't anyone come to the door? One of the blacks was speaking to him.

"What did you say?" Lennie asked.

"It's open. Just walk in."

"Oh, thank you," Lennie replied.

"It's all right. No charge," said the black man, and there was a lot of laughter and slapping of hands. Lennie had felt better playing billiards. But he walked on in anyway.

A girl, surprisingly modest and secretarial in appearance, a virtual ingenue blonde, faced him across a desk. Lennie by this time was *committed;* he would have walked through a gauntlet of his grandmother and a selection of elderly aunts to copulate with a fourteen-year-old cousin. Nonetheless he was reassured by the note of business as usual. He hoped he would get the receptionist; it would be like sleeping with his secretary, something everyone in the Political Science Department thought he did anyway. The girl gave him a card outlining the various massages—half hour, hour, one girl, two girls; he noticed it said TIPPING PERMITTED in bold caps at the bottom. That was new and reassuring. "I'll have an hour with one girl," he said.

She turned around and called through a curtain, "Tracy, Susie, we've got a customer." Tracy was a well-proportioned woman, with abundant red hair, whose breasts bulged over the top of a purple elastic bathing suit. Her skin was black, but her face had been powdered and she wore orange lipstick, to rhyme with her hair. She beamed at him as she entered. Susie was a white girl with fake blond hair. Her figure was nice enough, but when she smiled she showed discolored teeth that gave her a sickly look.

"Well, which one would you like?" the receptionist asked.

Lennie wanted to say, "You." But that didn't seem to be the program. He found himself gravitating toward the white girl. She had a vulnerable look that he liked and she looked younger than the other one. But then Lennie remembered all the conferences, protests, lectures, demonstrations. He remembered arguing long and bitterly with his wife over whether to send his son to private school. It might have been the beginning of their breakup. He had ended up calling her a bigot. She had replied that he was too tight even to spend a few thousand dollars of *her* money on the education of their own child—after he had made her send 500 dollars to some hopeless campaign in Mississippi.

"You don't have all *that* much money," he had replied.

It had not been a good move. She had pounced: "Well, I'm glad we've got the discussion down on your moral plane —my money."

So the boy had gone to private school. Ultimately Lennie had gone to Los Angeles, alone, to chase whores, with his own money, on his own moral plane. He decided that this was one time when he would have to be an equal opportunity employer.

He was reassured to find the rooms upstairs had locks. Tracy was all business. "Take off your clothes and get up on the table." Lennie complied. Tracy scattered powder here and there on his body and began to massage him: rubbing him well, probing and kneading his stiff shoulders, relaxing him for the first time during a whole evening of massages. Then he turned over on his back and Tracy bent her ample body, heavy with scent and suggestion, down over his. He began to feel stirrings of desire for her.

"Did you have anything else in mind, honey?" she asked. About five minutes of his hour had passed.

"Yes." His voice was very small now. "Could we ball?"

"Sure, honey, if you got fifty dollars."

"Yes, I got it," he said. He looked at her inquiringly. "I guess I should use one of these." There was a box of condoms on a small table by the door. He reached toward it.

"Well, honey, I got to *have* the fifty dollars, first. Right?" She looked at him appraisingly. "I don't do nothin' until I see the money."

He walked over to his pants, fumbled for his wallet, finally found it and fished for the right bills. He noticed that it was nearly all he had. He glanced back at her. She was stand-

ing there, in her suit, with her hands on her hips. He stood
naked under her gaze. He sucked in his stomach, inade-
quately, and he saw that she noticed. He had not felt less
sexual, without clothes, since his last prostate examination.
There was no way, he knew, that he could sleep with this
woman.

"God, I'm embarrassed," he said. "I don't seem to have
enough money."

"What you doin' talkin' 'bout ballin' when you ain't got
the money?" she said sourly. "How much *do* you have? I can
do other stuff, you know."

"I think I'd just like a plain massage and sauna," he said.

She looked at him coldly. "What's the matter with you?
Ain't *no*body come here for just a plain massage!" He felt it
coming and he knew it would hurt. "Ain't I good enough for
you?"

"Yes, yes," he said. "I really don't have the money for
anything big . . . Look I'll give you a tip anyway and go."

"Whatever you say, honey." He turned to the wall to
hide his wallet from her eyes and pulled out two tens and gave
them to her. She smiled. "You sure you don't want a massage?" she said.

"Yeah, I'm sure," he said. Feeling almost nauseated, he
asked where the sauna was. He felt that if he could sit in there
and sweat for a while, he could get rid of some of the sickness
in him, wash away his sense of corruption and bigotry and
impotence and fear, and go to some hotel and sleep well. She
pointed down a hall toward the center of the building. He
walked the length of the hall feeling conspicuous, and looked
through the window on the door. The light was on and there
was a smattering of pornographic magazines on the wooden
platform. His spirits lifted at the prospect of warmth. He remembered the balmy breeze at the airport. But when he
opened the door, the air inside was cool and clammy. He
didn't really consider complaining.

Later, he found Frank at the drugstore counter going

through the next day's L.A. *Times*. It said Nixon was unpopular, Mayor Bradley was fighting corruption, and the
Lakers were losing. Frank looked up at Lennie, raising his
eyebrows. "Another ripoff, huh?"

Lennie nodded. "Pretty much. Maybe we should have
gone to Love Unlimited."

"Well, you got any bright ideas for now, at three A.M.?"

"I guess we should go to a hotel. There's a motel right
down the street," Lennie said.

They walked out of the drugstore and down the street,
past the Pussycat Corral, past the Books of All Publishers
Arcade, past another police car, to the Siesta Motel on the
corner. The Siesta had telephones in every room, a swimming
pool, and for three dollars extra they would screen "XXX
adult" movies in the privacy of your room. Lenny and Frank
took a double to save money. Lennie wanted to swim but the
pool was closed. They decided not to order any movies.

It could be said that Frank and Lennie were both stupid
and unlucky. If you know where to look, it is not hard to find
a respectable whore in Los Angeles. Out-call services abound,
to judge from the advertisements, and one may guess that
the one entitled "The Human Orgasm" does not deal in
pocket billiards (though one never knows). There was even a
list of numbers available in the room at the Siesta Motel. It
was inscribed in neat handwriting on the last blank page, after
the .Book of Revelations, in the Gideon Bible. That is the
usual place. But it would not occur to Frank or Lennie to
seek guidance in a Bible.

They might have done better, too, by trying one of the
large selection of "personals" among the *Free Press* massage
displays, or in any other L.A. sex journal. One assumes that
these are essentially call girl ads. But Lennie and Frank did
not have a hotel room at the time and Frank wanted a sauna
and whirlpool to wash away the sediment of their impending
orgy. In addition, most attractive call girls are very expensive

and serve a dominantly married and wealthy clientele. The dregs and ripoffs are left for the compulsive bachelors.

If the professors had not been in such a hurry they could have waited a day and driven out to the Elysian Institute in Topanga Canyon, there to be connected to the world of middle-class swingers. But hurry and compulsiveness are the essence of the male sex drive. Most promising of all, perhaps, they could have taken their chances at the Civil Liberties conference. But they did not want to take chances.

There were many more reasonable things for them to do than spend some 350 dollars getting rubbed the wrong way by surly women in Los Angeles. But the sex business flourishes because men pursuing sex do not behave sensibly. If you put up a sign saying LOVE UNLIMITED and bathe it in purple light, they come like moths. You can get men to spend 50 dollars to sit on a couch and talk to a dull girl. You can get men to risk disease, robbery, and self-esteem sleeping with a streetwalker. You can get men to sit in the darkness and watch other people copulate with animals on a screen . . .

But the faith persists that through education and technology we are routinizing sex. Consider, for example, the critical reaction to *Our Time,* a sensitive and intelligent movie, set in 1956 in a girls' boarding school and written by Jane Stanton, who had been to one. In the film a girl gets pregnant and has to have an abortion. The sex tends to be clumsy and emotional. Everything is botched. Many critics, displaying their worldly knowledge, derided the story. Nothing like that, they said, could happen now, in the age of the Pill, among our liberated and sophisticated young.

But it happens. It happens every day. With the advent of legal abortions, birth control is bungled or forgotten more often than ever. Abortions themselves are increasingly used more than two times, which English data suggests may cause sterility. Venereal diseases are epidemic. And as any college psychologist will tell you, sex remains for many a perilous and traumatic matter. It remains particularly perilous and compulsive for single and divorced men.

Nonetheless, from the distance and safety of marriage and from the editorial offices of newspapers and magazines, sex among the young and the single often seems to resemble the promised land that opened up to Lennie and Frank, when they reached the middle pages of the L.A. *Free Press.* The purple lights still glow in the American night, and the moths still gather.

5

Revolutionary Hayrides

Although I have always suspected that life at its best is pushing the stone farther up the hill than anyone could have logically expected, eventually, over my dead body, perhaps we will all be one with one another, at ease on our planet, tensions gone.

But when there is no more guilt, mystery, conflict among us because we owe nothing, hide nothing—what will we dream of in the long days on the flattened hill?

—MARGOT HENTOFF

In understanding the predicament of single men it is important to assess the impact of the "Sexual Revolution" on their lives. But beyond the obvious advances in birth control and sexual "candor," the changes are often hard to find or define.

In reporting a revolution the usual place to begin is with the Public Relations Department—the Revolutionary press agents and writers. One may encounter them anywhere, particularly in New York. Assume, for example, that you are an attractive girl, briefly alone at a Manhattan cocktail party. A mousy, middle-aged man accosts you. He points to an attractive woman across the room. She is his wife, he says; she is "a wonderful and understanding woman." You do not know exactly what to say. You are happy for him. He then asks you to go to bed with him.

You look at him again. He seems vaguely familiar but you did not catch the name. Don't ask. The chances are ex-

traordinarily high—in fact, 100 percent among my acquaintances—that, yes, you have just been privileged to meet the
famous writer of that book on sex. You laugh incredulously
and say no. He immediately moves on to another woman.
Sexual revolutionaries have to cover a lot of ground. There
are not so very many of them.

That is one of the problems in appraising the Revolution.
When you approach Publicity Central, it says Research Institute on the door, and voices protest that there is no one in
here but us sociologists. When they speak, however, their
voices assume a seductive lilt and you'd better watch their
hands.

Another difficulty is that although many people like to
read about sexual revolutions, the ones who actually do it—
out there in Middle America—tend not to make very interesting reading. One of the most frequently cited exhibits of
sexual revolutionaries, for example, are the group of swingers
studied in Chicago by Gilbert Bartell.[1] Swingers are defined
as couples, chiefly married, who exchange sexual partners in
a systematic and impersonal way, without otherwise com-
promising the marriage or relationship. The Chicago group
would meet in a member's house, strip, and then go off to
bedrooms in pairs. Normally the man takes the initiative, and
each woman ends up sleeping with several of the men every
session. Each contact is limited to twenty minutes and there
are strict rules against making outside contact with partners
met in the process of swinging.

Bartell described this group as "middle class" and narrow
in their concerns. "We found," he wrote, "that they had no
outside activities or interests or hobbies . . . (they) did
nothing but swing and watch television. Yet a striking contrast is the fact that in their letters (questionnaires) they had
listed . . . travel, sports, movies, dancing, going out to dinner,
theater, etc. In fact they did none of these things. Therefore all conversational topics were related to swinging, swingers, and television programs."[2] Unless you are Joyce Carol

Oates, you are going to have trouble getting a best-seller out of that group. And unless you are George Wallace—one of their favorite politicians—you won't get them to tear anything down either, except clothing.

Writers about sexual revolution, however, are more interesting than their subjects. Lynn and James R. Smith, for example, are participant observers in the Sexual Revolution and co-directors of the Self Actualization Laboratory in Berkeley, California.[3] They are passionate advocates of let-it-all-hang-out, which they do often in their profession as sexual "therapists." People come from all over the country to learn from Lynn and James (tipping not permitted). "The conquest of sexual jealousy," they write, "could be the greatest advance in human relations since the advent of common law or the initiation of democratic processes." [4] That's the way they feel about it. What they are for is "a complex system and process of mutually negotiated and 'dyonomous' interaction which is, at least in part [mind you] metamotivated." Or, as they put it elsewhere, "the greater the liberality of opinion about pre-marital sexual intercourse the greater the likelihood of co-marital sex [adultery] ($X^2=107$, $df=15$, pl .001)," [5] and co-marital sex, they believe, can save the world.

As you might expect, deep thinkers like the Smiths would not have much patience with the Chicago group. But they even had a terrible time at Sandstone, the luxurious group sex facility in California, which holds large nude cocktail parties accompanied by sex, public and private. "Commercial treachery," the Smiths called it. "The men played characteristic sex roles and competed for the most desirable women . . . In many instances [these men and women] were acting as if they wanted to impress the others present with the fact that they were good enough to be there." [6]

So writers about sexual revolution normally do better writing about themselves than about the "revolutionaries," who all too often lack higher revolutionary "metamotivations." But in order to write about themselves and sexual revolution at the same time, they have to become "participant observers." Having read much of the recent literature on swinging, I suspect that there is as high a proportion of "participant observers" among America's swingers as F.B.I. informants in S.D.S.

It turns out that at a number of universities you can get a Ph.D. in sociology by going to sex orgies and asking questions. You can even get grants, and be published by major university presses. In fact, the Smiths' findings have been published by Johns Hopkins University Press in a compendium of studies on swinging called *Beyond Monogamy* and edited by Lynn and James. Among the contributors are George and Nena O'Neill (*Open Marriage*), Albert Ellis (*Sensuous Person: Critique and Corrections*), Jessie Bernard (*The Future of Marriage*), and Alex Comfort (*The Joy of Sex*). Comfort looks forward to the day when our society will transcend family and attain "universal kinship," affirmed by promiscuous sexual relations.[7]

Beyond Monogamy itself reveals this promiscuous principle at work in a more mundane way, in that the contributors continually cite one another's works. They present interesting data on some of the swinging clubs. We learn, for example, of revolutionary innovations: "Clubs such as 'Select,' 'Kindred Spirits,' 'Mixers,' and 'Swingers Life' have moved beyond the swingers' party to hayrides, and vacation trips."[8] We learn that although singles are nominally excluded from the Chicago group—along with couples with acne or otherwise "bad" complexions, i.e., blacks—one third of the participants are actually unmarried.[9] There is even a genuinely interesting article by Brian G. Gilmartin showing that the salient difference between a group of swingers and a normal control group in the California suburbs is the absence of close family ties among the swingers from the time of adolescence.[10]

What we do not learn from this 375-page study published by Johns Hopkins is the information we need to know to appraise the movement. The book does not tell us how many swingers there are. The Smiths estimate between one and eight million, which is another way of saying they don't have the slightest idea. Twitchell estimates 750,000.[11]

There is no evidence, however, that the actual movement of self-identified married "swingers"—as opposed to the singles, voyeurs, prostitutes, sado-masochists, homosexuals, and other deviant types who abound in "swinging advertisements" —comprises more than a 100,000 or so.

"Swinging," at least in the sense of partner exchanges and group sex, is obviously just a small part of what we mean when we speak of the Sexual Revolution. Even less extreme behavior could be termed revolutionary if it threatens basic institutions and relationships. Extramarital sex, premarital promiscuity, prolonged singleness, easy divorce—all might jeopardize traditional marriage and change the lives of single men.

Our sources of information on such sexual activities were greatly improved in the summer of 1974 with a re-markably forthright publication from agitprop central itself: *Playboy*. Entitled *Sexual Behavior in the 1970s* and written by Morton Hunt, the study presented the results of an ambitious national survey conducted by *Playboy* in 1972 with the assistance of the (Kinsey) Institute of Sex Research. Author of several previous books on sexual behavior, Hunt analyzed the new findings and compared them with the results of the two Kinsey Reports (1949 and 1954) and with other surveys of sexual conduct.[12]

The book begins with a slightly overwrought catalogue of "the sweep of change" ("By the end of 1972, an estimated 500 persons had undergone radical surgery and made the trans-sexual leap . . . it was becoming a commonplace" . . .).[13] But the real news is how little and how superficial much of the change appears to be. It would not be hard to conclude from Mr. Hunt's findings that the Sexual Revolution is really a media event—a matter of rotating styles—designed to sell books and magazines, plays and movies, rock stars and sex symbols: to keep the turnstyles revolving and the Revolution on stage—but having little traction in our inner lives. Yet such an assumption would be premature.

Although the age of first intercourse has gone down, young people today, he discovered, may well even be more likely than their elders to insist on sexual exclusiveness, and less likely to engage in sexual experiments with many partners before marriage. After marriage, they may be less likely than their elders to have extramarital affairs. Contrary to expectations, the acceptance of premarital intercourse has reaffirmed the conventions of monogamy. Rather than petting with lots of partners, teenaged girls now tend to sleep with one, and hope to marry him.

The range of petting has declined sharply since the time of Kinsey. While Kinsey's women had a median of eight petting partners, *Playboy*'s had just three. Including petting, Kinsey's women engaged in a wide circle of physical relationships for some six and a half years before marriage; *Playboy*'s settle down with one partner after three years. Most of *Playboy*'s group, 54 percent, claim to have had only one sex partner before marriage. Even in the younger section of the *Playboy* sample, more than half had had only one sex partner before marriage.[14]

Although a double standard persists, Hunt found that men have no more casual sex than a generation ago. Hunt concludes, "A growing body of research literature has established the fact that much of the current premarital coitus . . . takes place between males and females who live together in what are essentially trial marriages. . . ."[15] It is doubtful that this intensification of monogamous ties at an early age—to the exclusion of other relationships—leads to better marriages. But it clearly does not lead to casual or promiscuous activity.

After marriage a similar pattern obtains. "The picture is . . . one of very little change since Kinsey's time in the incidence of extra-marital behavior by males." Among women,

Playboy found no change in the number of extramarital partners and little over-all change in the likelihood of adultery. But in the youngest *Playboy* cohort, females under twenty-five, the women are rapidly closing the gap between them and the men. "A generation ago," Hunt writes, "only a third as many young wives as young husbands ventured outside of marriage; today, three quarters as many young wives as young husbands do so." [16] This change among the small minority of adulterous young people was the only significant breach in the double standard found in the Hunt statistics. In general, the *Playboy* poll and others show a reaffirmation and intensification of monogamous relationships. [17] There is reason to believe, moreover, that the current college generation is more conservative about sex than the late 1960s group studied by Hunt.

Jessie Bernard believes, however, that this renewed exclusiveness does not come without cost. There is a trade off between exclusiveness and permanence. The new generation has erected higher standards of sexual monogamy, but it pays for them with diminished prospects for durability. [18] While the Kinsey sample was so committed to preserving their union that they would tolerate greater violation of it, the new generation is more willing to break up if their marriage goes bad. (It may be that as their marriages expand into families, much of the new group will adopt an attitude more closely corresponding to the old one.)

While there is some truth in this reasoning, it seems inadequate as an explanation for the rising divorce rate, at least among the young. An extended period of sleeping with one partner may lead to premature monogamy while the longer period of petting and playing the field in the past allowed people to meet a wider variety of possible spouses. The Hunt statistics indicate that the slightly later age of marriage today is very deceptive. It conceals the fact that the effective moment of choice is fully three years younger than it used to be in the 1940s and 1950s. This "revolution" can also be seen as a disguised return to the teenage marriages of previous centuries.

These findings only strengthen the key conclusions of the *Playboy* poll. Monogamy remains the central value of our sex lives. In this regard, the United States resembles all other major industrial countries. Even in notorious Sweden—which has usurped France in American sexual daydreams—93 percent of the population opposes extramarital affairs.[19] Sweden is an interesting example, because that nation adopted a custom of late marriages and intense monogamous premarital activity well before the United States. Many observers misinterpreted this pattern as a sign of promiscuity and moral breakdown. Long experience in Sweden and considerable experience here has begun to refute this connection. Disturbing things may be happening in both the United States and Sweden with regard to sex. But premarital activity, itself, is probably not a significant problem, except when it occurs at a very young age.

Another ostensible part of the sexual revolution is the movement of physical sex, copulation, to the very center of our lives, in an explicit and conscious way. As Hunt dramatizes, there has been a vast expansion of public sexual display —what is called "sexual candor"; a large increase in the incidence of sexual activity, chiefly monogamous, whether in or out of wedlock; and a significant spread in the knowledge and use of varying sexual techniques. The *Playboy* survey dwells rather heavily on the "new" positions and techniques (most of which go back to the Pleistocene age).

But the sexual rewards of this change are uncertain at best. Despite all the furor, despite the nationwide publication of the rules (no longer can a couple fall innocently into the game of love without a knowledge of its "goal"), and despite the injection of a mechanical scoreboard in the consciousness of every boy and girl, women have orgasms scarcely more often than in the days of Kinsey. Only 53 percent of current wives have orgasm all or almost all of the time, compared to

45 percent of the wives in the Kinsey survey.[20] These results accord with the findings of Seymour Fisher's study for The National Institutes of Health [21] and with a *Redbook* poll of 500,000 women, also in 1972, except that Fisher and *Redbook* indicated virtually no change at all from the Kinsey data.[22]

Any gains, moreover, cannot be ascribed to revolution. In extramarital intercourse, Hunt found, only 39 percent of the women usually had orgasm, while 35 percent almost never did, a rate of failure five times higher than in marital sex (7 percent). In addition, the sexual technique best correlated with high orgasmic success is not often recommended highly by the sexual revolutionaries. It is to stay married fifteen years—the amount of time it took to reach the *Playboy* survey level.[23]

Fisher's study found orgasmic success most likely when a woman trusts that her lover will not leave.[24] Prostitutes, reportedly, almost never have orgasms, except by masturbating. One wonders whether the orgasm scoreboard—like a pinball machine—contains a Tilt mechanism. If you probe and palpate the sensorium too much—without love—the woman turns off. So whatever are the effects of liberated positions and techniques, female orgasm does not seem to be one of them.[25] Sexual revolution may be better at producing impotence than orgasm.

A further weakness of the Sexual Revolution, is its infestation with crab lice and venereal diseases. As the orgiast awakens the next morning, basking in the glow of his memories, he discovers that there were ants at the picnic. It is really a dreadful disappointment to him. He knows he will have to go to a doctor to get a special prescription, because the new breeds of sexual revolutionary lice eat Pyrenex 400 for breakfast. He knows he will then have to soak or boil his clothes and sheets. He knows he will have to drench himself in a noxious oil. Then he knows he will have to wait and see. Half the time the little bastards come back.

When there are crab lice, moreover, there are apt to be other infections, also combat ready. The cases of syphilis are relatively rare. But new strains of gonorrhea, some of them imported from Vietnam and resistent to penicillin and other antibiotics, are epidemic. Our orgiast looks for symptoms. Normally he finds them after a while. But he is not sure, for psychosomatic venereal disease is nearly as prevalent as the real infection. Back he goes to the doctor for tests, pills, or shots. Increasingly, these days, however, he discovers he has Herpes Simplex II, a chronic viral infection, associated to a chilling degree with cervical cancer. There is no cure for Herpes; just like cold sores, the infection can break out at any time; then it goes dormant, only to return. It can cause birth defects and spontaneous abortions if present at the cervix or in the vagina. A pregnant woman with an active infection often must have a caesarian section. Two hundred and fifty thousand cases of Herpes Simplex II arise annually.[26] The various forms of venereal disease together account for millions of infections a year. Any promiscuous person is likely to get one. These problems affect single men more than any other group, since single women are less promiscuous. But those seeking equal rights in the Revolution are getting their share.

Over-all, we find once again that even in the realm of philandering, it is the married men who are resourceful enough to find healthy, unpromiscuous women, or swing with healthy couples. As in the case of poverty, crime, mental illness, depression, and mortality, it is the single men who are the casualties of Sexual Revolution. Though they are more promiscuous, they also have less total sexual experience than monogamous men or women. As Hunt shows, in the younger age groups single men only have about one fifth as much sexual activity as married men of the same age, and less than half as much sexual activity as single females.[27] Single men are also less successful on the inner scoreboard—women's orgasms. But being most promiscuous it is the single males who are most prone to venereal disease, most likely to be impotent or sexually violent.

Single men between twenty and forty increased by 1,500,000 between 1970 and 1973, most of them near the peak marital age of between 23 and 26,[28] while the number of single women rose only 600,000.[29] There will not be enough single women to go around for several years. Nearly a million of them have been taken by older divorced men.

Single Menace

Virtue will never exist so long as there are men who scorn the laws of nature, carrying scandal into society and shame and despair into families; he who does not marry, although normally constituted, cannot in general be virtuous, because organized like anyone else, he seeks victims everywhere . . . he introduces into society the germs of the passions which sooner or later must subvert it.

> *Comité de Legislation, societé revolution-*
> *naire de Sens* (1794)

One Sunday in early 1974, the Washington *Post* caused a big furor by introducing its readers to a young man named Stuart Brauer. Brauer is tall, blond, blue-eyed, and single. He has, as he described it, a Porsche "like a silver bullet," fourteen pairs of "current, in-fashion, hip, high style, high platform shoes," and "an average of three foxy chicks a week."[1]

Brauer is admittedly something special. For one thing, he is a "double Scorpio." "That's a very physically oriented sign," he explains, "and I exemplify it one hundred percent. The physical aspect is necessary if you want to take one of the Brauer boys off the street for a night." Since this Brauer boy dates hundreds of women yearly and turns them over rapidly, he is not exactly an impossible dream, if you are a Washington girl with a "physical aspect" and a good turnover.

But let the *Post* describe Mr. Brauer. It does him well, using the idiom of a Dewars whiskey advertisement: [2]

NAME: Stuart C. Brauer
HOME: Alexandria, Va.
AGE: 27
PROFESSION: Sales manager for Xerox Corporation, in charge of achieving in excess of $4 million per year in revenue.
HOBBIES: Jetty fishing, skeet shooting, pheasant hunting— "I especially like ladies who know how to put one together with orange sauce"—and skiing. "After ten days at Aspen, Stowe and Killington are gar-baaage. I wouldn't waste a dime there."
LAST BOOKS READ: *The Godfather, The Exorcist.* "If my arm is twisted about a good book I'll read it."
LAST ACCOMPLISHMENT: Arriving in Houston for the Super Bowl, "The very first thing I did, I didn't even go up to my room, was ask the bellhop for the nearest lounge with the finest chicks. And as I walked in I saw this solid stick of dynamite that absolutely knocked me out. I said, 'You are out of sight, when are we going to get together?' And in the four days I was there we put a program together that could make a book."
QUOTE: "A turtle is born with the instinct to walk toward the water, and Stuart Brauer was born with the instinct to go after skirts."

So Stuart Brauer is a successful single man, or, to be specific, a successful divorced man, since—like most successful men—he has been married. He is a product of money, and a culture that defines masculinity chiefly in terms of sexual prowess. His essential values prevail among millions of young males, and inform our best-selling magazines for men. Brauer boys will diminish in number only when there is a depression —in money, or in sex as the remaining masculinity rite.

But the playboy is not the only ascendant style of American manhood. Elsewhere in the same issue of the Washington *Post* is an essay by novelist Larry McMurtry about another kind of young man. McMurtry's group, unlike the Brauer boys, shrink from the sexual arena. They have rejected, McMurtry maintains, the playboy's attempt "to be beautiful and to be desired."

"One cannot visit many campuses today," McMurtry writes, "without feeling that young men have already abandoned that aim and retreated several more steps . . . boys and girls alike talk of sexual rejection with the seriousness with which middle-aged people might talk of terminal cancer. . . . The girls can hardly enjoy their budding independence because of the fear that in the process of keeping it they will seriously damage if not completely crush the invariably frail masculine egos they must deal with, and one gets the sense that many of them spend a lot of time trying to think of ways to keep these . . . flowerlets from being deposited in their hands." [3]

Let us try another Dewars ad:

NAME: Byron Glass

HOME: Darien, Connecticut

AGE: 27

PROFESSION: Songwriter for "Cosmic Trust," a defunct rock group.

HOBBIES: Photography, record collecting, meditation— "Man, sometimes I'm going along and I see a *flower* beside the road and it really knocks me out, man, you know what I mean?"—and music—"Sometimes I wish I didn't give up the piano when I was a kid."

LAST BOOKS READ: *Stranger in a Strange Land* and *The Godfather.* "I dig books. Like I'll read anything, man."

LAST ACCOMPLISHMENT: "I went up to Watkins Glen and like, man, I didn't even hear the fuckin' music, man, I was so spaced out, man, this chick I was with thought I was dying. She was *weird,* man. I wasn't

dyin', I was flyin'! I must have tripped for two whole
days. Man, I should have written a song about it, you
know what I mean?"

QUOTE: "Everybody is hassling me all the time to get a
job. Now I'd like to work at something groovy, man.
Like I could manage a rock group or be a disk jockey
or sell records or something. I might write a novel
though, you know what I mean?"
or
"The lemming is born with the instinct to join a
crowd and walk toward the water but I'd rather just
sit here and bloom in the sunlight . . . Winter?
Shit man, I don't pay any mind to that establishment
bullshit."

Like the Brauer image, the notion of fragile flowerlets
seems a bit exaggerated. Still, recent sex research offers startling evidence of a sexual crisis among young men, marked
by sexual fragility and retreat. A *Playboy* survey of college
students in 1971 indicated that while virginity among girls
was rapidly diminishing, virginity among boys was actually
increasing, and at an equal rate. Greater female availability
and aggressiveness often seems to decrease male confidence
and initiative.

Further evidence of a flowerlet syndrome comes in the
form of impotence. Impotence has become the leading com-
plaint at virtually every college psychiatric clinic. Psychiatrist
Harvey E. Kaye calls it "the least publicized epidemic of the
last decade." He cites evidence from "my patients, both male
and female," "articles in medical journals," and "conversa-
tions with my colleagues." [4] While Kinsey's 1949 study indicated impotence problems in only 1.3 percent of men under
thirty-five, a 1970 poll by *Psychology Today* reported one in
three men with erectile difficulties.[5] Both surveys used skewed
samples: Kinsey's had an excess of prisoners; *Psychology
Today*'s had too many of its own subscribers. But, whatever
the objective situation, there seems little doubt that impotence

has greatly increased as a subjective concern of American men.

As an additional grim entry on the sexual scene—to go with the playboys and flowerlets—we have an expanding number of rapists. Although dignified married men with high status in their communities receive the most publicity, rape is another specialty of single men with confused sexual identities. Proportionately, a single man is five times as likely as a married man to be convicted of rape. The reported incidence of this crime increased almost 80 percent between 1968 and 1974, and the real incidence probably increased also.[6]

Like impotence, however, the subjective impact of rape grew even more strikingly than its measurable occurrence, with a proliferation of "rape control centers," study groups, magazine articles, books, and legislative proposals. We even had the emergence of retroactive "political rape," as Eldridge Cleaver sought to dignify his criminal past; and the concept of "consensual rape" as Germaine Greer sought to redefine the art of seduction. With a decline in plot and character in the movies, rape also became an essential part of the film makers' repertory. Combining shock and titillation, sex and violence, it provided a valuable alternative to talent and intelligence for many a director of the late 1960s and early 70s.

So we have the playboy, the impotent, and the rapist as an unholy trinity of single manhood. Together they comprise only a minority of all single men; they are the superstuds, the defenseless, the violent, the most conspicuous winners and most abject losers of the Sexual Revolution. But they play a much larger role in the consciousness of our time. They offer the appeal of demonic darkness, as strong as the orgiastic light itself, to those who gather on mountaintops and dream of the end of sexual rules and limitations: the end to monogamy.

The dream of liberation from monogamy emerges in a chorus of influential voices. They speak in terms of "freedom" and "fulfillment." Books like *Beyond Monogamy,* magazines like *Playboy,* organizations like the Humanists and the Sexual

Freedom League, all present themselves as embattled "liberals" confronting a powerful and reactionary establishment. The sexual liberals purport to be "the open," "the creative," the "genitally liberated" facing the "repressives," "the paranoids," the "anal compulsives." The liberals are against power games and for the sharing of love. As Alex Comfort has put it, they are for "universal kinship," and equality.

Why then is the real effect of their scheme the emergence of impotents, playboys, and rapists? The reason is that the removal of restrictions on sexual activity does not bring equality and community. It brings ever more vicious sexual competition. The women become "easier" for the powerful to get—but harder for others to keep. Divorces become "easier," but remarriage is extremely difficult for abandoned older women. Marriages become more "open"—open not only for the partners to get out but also for the powerful to get in.

Monogamy is central to any democratic social contract, designed to prevent a breakdown of society into "war of every man against every other man." In order to preserve order, a man may relinquish liberty, prosperity, and power to the state. But if he has to give up his wife to his boss, he is no longer a man. A society of open sexual competition, in which the rich and powerful—or even the sexually attractive—can command large numbers of women is a society with the most intolerable hierarchy of all. In any polygamous society some men have no wives at all. Men denied women and children are deprived of the very substance of life.

Monogamy is egalitarianism in the realm of love. It is a mode of rationing. It means one to a customer. Competition is intense enough even so, because of the sexual inequality of human beings. But under a regime of monogamy there are limits. One does not covet one's neighbor's wife. One does not leave one's own when she grows older, to take a woman who would otherwise go to a younger man. A single man does not long dissipate a woman's child-bearing years, for they will never return for her. Thus a balance is maintained and each generation gets its only true sexual rights: the right to one wife or husband and the right to participate in the future of the race through children.

It is not a ruthlessly strict system. Many divorces among the young are relatively harmless. There is a place in the system for some philandering. But the essential rules are necessary to a just and democratic society. A breakdown in the sexual order will bring social ills and injustices far more grievous than the usual inequalities of money and power.

Such a breakdown is already occurring in American society. The most obvious evidence is the ever-growing number of older divorcées. Between the ages of forty and sixty-five, there were 1,600,000 divorced women in 1973, up 231,000 since 1970, while there were only 935,000 divorced men.[7] The divorced men, moreover, were remarrying over three times as fast as the divorcées.[8] This disparity is caused by a fundamental inequality between the sexes.

Unlike divorced men, most of whom find wives within a few years, women over forty only rarely remarry. The median age for these divorced women was approximately forty, while the median age for the women whom the men took as their second wives was about thirty.[9] A woman divorced after forty—after her child-bearing years—is most likely to spend the rest of her life unmarried. Although women in general can bear singleness far better than can men, this huge number of divorcées is a national tragedy.

A society is an organism. We cannot simply exclude a few million women from the fabric of families, remarry their husbands to younger women, and quietly return to our business as if nothing has happened. What has happened is a major rupture in the social system, felt everywhere.

Older divorced women are not the only victims of this rupture. The other victims are young single men. When the divorced men marry young women, the older men, in effect, become polygamists. Each man monopolizes the fertile, eligible years of two or more women. The inevitable result is that millions of young single men cannot get married or have children.

Between twenty and forty, there are 1,250,000 more single, separated, or divorced men than single, separated, and divorced women.[10] When the million or so divorced and separating men between forty and fifty-five enter the fray—to remarry women with a median age in their low thirties—the strains are intense. Eighty-five percent of the women between twenty-five and forty are already married.[11] The ones who are single in many cases are not eager to get married or are unlikely prospects for some other reason. Many single women over thirty are earning substantial incomes and are unwilling to marry less successful men. Thus the field for the single men is diminished still further.

The over-all result is sexual pressure on most men and most marriages. It is sexual turbulence and struggle extended throughout the society. It is fatherless children and childless fathers. It is a rising incidence of homosexuality, a frequent recourse of marginal males in polygamous societies everywhere. Above all, the result is an abundance of losers, men and women lost in the sexual shuffle and relegated to the singles game, in which almost no one wins.

So few win because the losers of the sexual revolution—post-forty women and young men—cannot marry each other. The divorced women are too old and the single men too young. Although women's magazines have long been entertaining their readers with happy stories of sex between these two available generations, the cases of marriage are extremely rare. The few marriages that do occur between young men and older divorced women, moreover, do not often bring children or real family responsibilities. The young man is only technically married.

The fact remains that young men almost always marry women of child-bearing age. By and large, single men of all ages fall in love with young women. When they fail to find young single women, they prospect among the married ones.

If they fail here, they do not get married at all. It is the same with older divorced men. They will often marry a teeny-bopper before a woman their own age or older.

Throughout human evolution the competition among men has focused on fertile women. That is the very essence of the male sex drive. Outside of literature, men are not usually attracted sexually to women whose age reminds them of their mothers. Even when children are not consciously sought, men are most attracted to women who can bear them; and children are still a vital, if often unconscious motive of marriage.

The chief beneficiaries of sexual revolution, therefore, are older, married men with exceptional appeals and powers. They can leave their older wives and marry younger ones. In addition, powerful men can have young mistresses, thus dominating two young women. These forms of polygamy create a large number of peripheral males who cannot win a durable relationship with a woman and whose existing ties are always in jeopardy. As in a baboon troop, the powerful get the women most of the time; and the powerful father most of the children.

It is then that the peripheral men feel sexually expendable. But, unlike the peripheral baboons, who are physically controlled by the dominant ones, the peripheral men are not powerless. They can buy knives and guns, drugs and alcohol, and thus achieve a brief and predatory dominance or an illusory potency. The rapist, the addict impotent, and Stuart Brauer, in a way become equals.

It should be remembered that the real arenas of sexual revolution in America are not the universities, but the black ghettos. Although statistics are not available for the ghetto itself, the over-all black totals are heavily influenced by ghetto conditions. Thirty-nine percent of all black men are single, compared to 27 percent of white men.[12] Only 52 percent of black children under eighteen are living with both parents, down 7 percent in three years, to a level 35.8 points below the white percentage.[13] Black women, through jobs and welfare, tend to be financially independent of the men. In the ghetto divorce and desertion are more common than anywhere else in the society, and sexual competition and bravado are as pervasive as at Sandstone.

But the ghetto does not provide a secure place for the losers, a secure haven of love and self-esteem. The ghetto often cannot enforce monogamy or perpetuate marriage. So most older ghetto women lack husbands. So half the violent crimes in America are committed by and against ghetto residents. So rape and impotence, addiction and robbery all too often cast a pall over the streets and homes. In the ghetto the Stuart Brauers become pimps and command the scene; the impotents become addicts and waste away; the rapists remain at large; and the women grow old without husbands.

Even though there are many reasons for the ghetto tragedy—both in our history and in our current policy—there is no doubt that it has now assumed the bitter pattern of sexual emancipation. It is the losers' side of the Sexual Revolution. People who would like to extend the pattern to the rest of the society should study it well.

They also might study the Moslem world and other polygamous societies. The results are suppression of women and the emasculation of single men—the emergence of large numbers of homosexuals. The sexual order becomes more rigid and oppressive than the worst liberationist caricature of the American small town.

The sexual liberal, with his talk of love and sharing and universal kinship, sounds like a rather conventional utopian: sentimental but harmless, and with his heart in the right place. In fact, however, the sexual revolutionary is more dangerous than most, because his program is at once less realistic and more feasible. Unlike the economic or political utopia, the sexual one can be practiced in one's own home. But also unlike the economic or political utopian, who at least gestures at realities of scarcity and interdependence, the sexual liberal rarely transcends the womb-world of his own imagination. In theory, his program is utterly misconceived, and in practice it is evil.

Even a communist, for example, knows that equality takes work, power, even dictatorship. He has no illusion that freedom alone will achieve it. That is why ·the communist conception of freedom is so nebulous and collective. But to the sexual revolutionary it goes without saying that people become' equal merely by taking off their clothes. It is a surprising variation on the theory, never really believed even by its proponents, that "they're all the same in the dark."

Yet the descriptions of swinging in *Beyond Monogamy* offer abundant sociological data, for those who reject the evidence of their own lives and senses, that sexual appeal is no more equally distributed than anything else. One might go further. Sexual appeal is distributed with an unevenness more inexorable and irreversible than almost any other human advantage—perhaps even more than intelligence and virtue, certainly more than money and power.

On the most obvious level, older men are much more powerful sexually than older women, and younger, fertile women are much more powerful sexually than younger men. But inequalities in sexual appeal are great among men and women of all ages.

Monogamy is designed to prevent the powerful of either sex from disrupting the familial order. In practice, however, the chief offenders are older men. Young women, however powerful sexually, do not normally want to exercise their powers to gain large numbers of partners.

Female sexuality, in fact, forms the last line of defense for sexual morality. Women's desire for long-term ties is reinforced by a range of differences between the sexes. One can say that women have a real biological need for monogamy, while men have to be taught to repress their polygamous impulses.

The women's sex drive is not usually short term and copulatory; it embraces the rich physical events of maternity.

The man has only one sex act, intercourse, and a more compulsive need to perform it with whomever is immediately available.

Women's orgasms are partly dependent on a reliable partner, a partner who will stay. Men's are not.

Women want to know the father of their children. Men may be far away when their children are born.

Women become pregnant, feel vulnerable, want protection. Men do not have these experiences.

Women labor and bear children, nurture them, sense their terrible fragility, see the need for a stable society. The men's connection to children is more tenuous and is granted by the women.

Women grow old and know they can no longer bear children, no longer compete for men; they want their husbands to stay with them. Men remain fertile, and sometimes attractive to younger women; they can fantasize a lifetime of philandering.

As repeated polls have shown, women are strikingly less interested in competition, dominance, and power than are men. One man is normally enough for a woman.

Men, too, have a desperate need for enduring relationships with women. But they often don't know it, so they are most likely to entertain dreams of sexual revolution, in which they can live their fantasies of continual sexual conquest.

Female resistance to sexual revolution has been repeatedly demonstrated. Attempts to promote communal sex usually leave women cold. H. Wayne Gourley, for example, established "Walden Two" as a utopian community in Pennsylvania partly to experiment with group marriage. But in the end he had to leave the group and sell his house to it. The experiment failed, according to Kathleen Greibe's report, because "There has never been a female at Walden House who had any interest at all in group marriage." [14] This is not a surprising fact. According to anthropologists, there has never been any group of women who have long permitted a regimen of group sex. Group sex has occurred chiefly when powerful men have enforced it.

Nonetheless, this crucial female desire for monogamy, though biologically deep, can be culturally overcome. The society, through its media and other propaganda, can create social pressures that break down the women's resistance. Women have greater orgasmic capacity than men and can be taught to use it widely. Then you can have, in some communities, a sexual revolution.

Any sexual revolution, however, will tend to liberate more men than women. The woman's biological tendency toward monogamy and responsibility for children will have an effect. Larger numbers of men than women will command two or more exclusive partners. Thus a sexual revolution will exclude many more young men than young women. In addition, any older woman with a sexually attractive husband is likely to be deserted. When the society stops enforcing monogamy, a social order based on monogamous families will break down into a system based on the bitter hierarchies of sexual power.

Such disasters of sexual inequality explain why real egalitarians, even revolutionary ones like Fidel Castro and Mao Tse-tung are normally conservative about sex. They do not want to liberate its disruptive and hierarchical potentials. That is why libertarians, who even want to turn the police force over to private enterprise, hesitate to extend *laissez faire* to sex. That is why the program of the sexual revolution—with its promised link of freedom and equality—is even more fatuous, more quixotic, than any of the long procession of egalitarian dreams that have bemused this century's politics. Sexual liberals and revolutionaries are anything but egalitarians. They are just men with sexual ambition or dreams of orgiastic glory. The women who are foolish enough to support them are anything but true "feminists." Sexual revolutionary women are most often the dupes of the *Playboy* philosophy.

Forget equality. What you get when you liberate sex is

power. What you get is a vast intensification of sexual competition, from which there is no sure haven except impotence
and defeat; competition in which marriage is just another
arena, or the home base from which the strong deploy; competition in which the only sure result is an ever larger band of
vindictive losers.

In some societies, losers do not matter very much. They
can be sent to rest homes and asylums, dispatched to distant
wars, or thrown in jail. But the success or failure of a peaceful democratic society is dependent on what happens to the
people who lose. To say that most people can live with sexual
"liberation" is irrelevant if it creates a class of real revolutionaries and criminals, irrelevant if it deprives large numbers of
people of the essentials of human dignity and love.

7

Immaculate Evolution

The recurrent problem of civilization is to define the male role . . . .

—MARGARET MEAD

It is one of the more persistent human traits. It may even be part of our capacity for greatness—our ability as a species repeatedly to transcend what we are. Scopes discovered it some fifty years ago when he got it in his head to teach Darwin in the public schools of Dayton, Tennessee. Others have discovered it since, in circles more sophisticated. Human beings—particularly the higher-minded sorts—do not enjoy being reminded of their kinship with the animals. They do not, in fact, even like to be told of their kinship with their own bodies. In particular, they do not like imagining that their spiritual faculties, their minds, are in any very important way connected to their bones and glands and alimentary canals.

Yet we are appraising the condition of single men—men who only rarely transcend what they are. With them, at least, one notices quickly that, if anything, their brains are keener on serving their bodies than the other way around; and when they open their mouths, it is often their glands and hungers as much as their minds that tend to speak. In any case, it is extraordinarily difficult to separate mind and body and probably unwise to try (except in a metaphysical or religious sense), since the result is likely to be a general weakening of

81

all faculties, followed in rather short order by death. Enough single and divorced men are dying already.

Clarence Darrow in losing his famous "monkey trial" battle with William Jennings Bryan must have looked forward to a day of vindication. As the jury disbanded and poor Mr. Scopes went off to jail, and Darrow went back to Chicago, and Bryan went into decline—and the apes were relieved of responsibility for any of it—there must have been wry amusement in intellectual circles (and considerable jubilation in the jungle). Such things were to be expected from small Tennessee towns. But the day would come when science would illumine the back side of the moon, even the dark reaches of the Cumberlands; when empirical truth would dispel the clouds of fundamentalist religion.

Of course, the day did come. The champions of scientific truth are now in command. It is now acknowledged that human beings, like any other of nature's creatures, are products of evolution. The story of Genesis is recognized as a myth— first as a beautiful one, now increasingly as a "sexist" one— but, at best, as a parable of dubious import. Man is known to be an animal, a mammal, a primate, and a hominid, in that order.

So we set Scopes free. But before he returns to the classroom there are a few things for him to learn: in truth, a new fundamentalism of enlightenment. It will seem surprisingly familiar to him. In fact, he may wonder whether his old Darwinian protest has been vindicated at all. The new vision of man, widely advocated in sociology, anthropology, and psychology, is almost identical to the one adduced by William Jennings Bryan. There is a new Genesis.

Like the old, it separates man from evolutionary heredity and the animal kingdom. Like the old, it envisages a tree of knowledge that displaces the tree of evolution. The language of the social engineer is more unctuous and ambiguous than the Bible. But he expresses the same desire to see man as immaculately conceived and thus infinitely malleable: perfectible. Of course, the gods are new, but they are as unpleasant as some of the old ones, and they do not permit any more freedom (free will) to monkey around. If man is an evolutionary blank, those in control of environment can inscribe any tyranny they wish.

Once Scopes has mastered the new revelation, he can even return to the remaining old fundamentalists back in the hills and reassure them. Yes, Scopes will admit, man evolved from the apes. But it didn't make any difference. You see, a miraculous event occurred! "Yes, Lord," they can respond. Quite suddenly in the long sweep of time we were given this huge brain, so unique among all the beasts and birds that it permanently separated us from them, giving us a higher mentality that might even be called, if one prefers the term, soul. "Hallelujah."

What we have here is nothing less than a doctrine of immaculate evolution. If one is an old fundamentalist, one can ascribe the change to divine will. If one is a new fundamentalist, one can guess that it was something we ate—apples, perhaps. If one wishes to join the two possibilities, we can agree that the apples of this tree of knowledge were divine.

In any case, the result will not be disputed in the Cumberlands. The new Genesis renders man a unique and separate being, related to the animals only in merely physical ways. Man was set free of the limits and necessities of the animal world. One could even say he was expelled from the garden of nature and made master of the earth.

Why was man set free in this manner? The old fundamentalist can easily answer that question. He was set free of nature and given dominion over the birds and beasts so that he could do the will of God. Here the new fundamentalist balks, for he is a stickler for words and he doesn't like the word "God." He would say man was set free of nature and made master of it so that he could create a better world.

As a cultural animal and an adaptive one, he can perfect himself and his environment. But what does he adapt to? He adapts to his environment through his culture. But isn't he master of his environment? He is getting there. Then is he not, in essence, creating himself? Exactly. But in what image? The image of reason, compassion, and truth to be attained by our most visionary citizens. Where do they get this vision? Well, there is man's big brain, his soul, his cortical miracle, that allows him to see what should be done. Rather than say, "Do the will of God," say simply, "Do good," or "Do Good" (if not, "Do God").

Here the whole fundamentalist apple cart, old and new, will collide with the evolutionary tree, and apples of knowledge rather than monkey fur, will fly. Anyone who tries to create a good society that does not conform to the evolutionary nature of man will fail. Human beings are specific animals with histories and limits, possibilities and propensities, and their brain, as well as many of their social usages and institutions, evolved like everything else.

Cultures, too, are evolutionary products, but of a different kind. Specific cultures are varying expressions of heredity and environment as they interact in society. Innate propensities—such as sexuality, aggression, love, and competition—can emerge in many different ways. They can be constricted or suppressed or sublimated or fulfilled or exaggerated or refined, as a specific society chooses. But human nature cannot be ultimately denied without fostering tendencies of failure and disintegration, or reducing and destroying the essence of humanity.

This knowledge gives man the dignity of a specific nature. He must be fathomed and respected if the society is to work. He is not infinitely malleable, manipulable, perfectible. He is not a blank—or punch card—on which can be inscribed any program that the powerful conceive, however good. He is an enormously complex, endlessly fascinating, marvelously ingenious and resourceful being, with an ultimately particular and refractory nature. He lives in societies that must in great degree accord with that nature because they evolved in interaction with it. Anyone who wants to improve the lot of man—with whatever high project—should respect him enough to find out who he most essentially is.

This, of course, is a moral injunction. For in a totalitarian age, it may be possible to break down and destroy man—neutralize him, adapt him, lobotomize him. He is irreducible, perhaps, only as long as one insists that he be a man. If one envisions a larger schema—a more exalted order, a more esthetic pattern—than men and women can naturally accept, then one can put them in a zoo, break their spirits, and teach them the higher truth. A procrustean science can inject them, sculpt them, as it wishes and create a "new man." He won't, however, be a free man.

In a sense, all men are, for a time, single men. In another sense, before marriage became paramount, most of the warrior and hunting history of human kind was forged by single men. In exploring the roots of the single male predicament today, one finds oneself exploring the sources of modern society itself. And one contemplates the enigma of what we consider maturity in men.

Such a venture is necessarily speculative, even poetic. Some of the most compelling works in this field have been offered by former playwright Robert Ardrey, author of the formidable trilogy, *African Genesis, The Territorial Imperative,* and *The Social Contract.*[1] Citing a wealth of new archeological data, Ardrey weaves a powerful argument that man evolved during millions of years as a carnivorous hunter on the African savannahs, and that our most authentic ancestor was a killer ape.

One of Ardrey's valuable contributions was to flush into publication one Elaine Morgan, also a playwright, and author of *The Descent of Woman.*[2] She believes that our killer ape was marinated and modified during the some ten million years of the Pliocene, when Africa was ravaged with drought. The hominid, she assumes, was driven to the sea, where it became an amphibious creature, subsisting on clams and such, losing its hair, and developing a brain and speech capability more like a dolphin's than a monkey's. To many professionals, of course, such speculation is simply a rather immoral way of making money.

Beyond all such hypotheses, we are left with the indubitable proposition that evolving hominids engaged for some millions of years in hunting and gathering. We may further assume, from both archeological and anthropological evidence, that men did almost all the hunting and women did most of the gathering. Human beings became one of the most dimorphic of all beasts, with large differences between the sexes, not only in the reproductive systems but also in size, body weight, muscular development, fat distribution, skeletal formation, hair, and hormones.

The hunting party was typically a group of cooperating males. We know this both from current anthropological evidence and from the piles of large animal bones that have been found in caves with hominid fossils in southern Africa. One man alone with rudimentary weapons could not have brought down a wildebeest. There evolved, as a result, a strong human propensity to form all-male groups for purposeful and often hazardous activity. This tendency survived into agricultural societies, where it was not really needed except for defense.

Yale anthropologist David Pilbeam has shown, in fact, that male insistence on sex segregation of roles actually increases as it becomes less necessary, and thus more open to challenge. He compares groups of hunting Bushmen in Africa with groups who have moved onto farms. "Among Bushmen who are still hunters," he writes,

> sex roles are far from rigid, and in childhood the two sexes have a very similar upbringing. However, among those Bushmen who have adopted a sedentary life devoted to herding or agriculture, sex roles are much more rigid. Men

devote their energies to one set of tasks and women to another, mutually exclusive set. Little boys learn only "male"
tasks and little girls exclusively female ones.[3]

This pattern, found among the Bushmen, a most pacific
and cooperative hunting society, is repeated worldwide in
the annals of anthropology. Lionel Tiger has developed an
elaborate argument that the resulting tendency of men to bond
with one another in purposeful and often aggressive groups
precedes even the male–female tie itself. The closest tie in
virtually all societies, primate and human, is between women
and children. But the next most common and strong connection may well be the all-male bond. The translation of the
rudimentary impulse of love into intense ties between specific
men and women appears to have been emphasized and sancti-
fied later, in the course of creating civilized societies.

Whether for hunting or defense, the all-male group leads
an erratic existence. It goes on chases that climax in battle.
It rises to occasions of furious activity. Then it subsides for
days of torpor. When he lacks a clear, immediate stimulus or
a profound, long-term goal, the human male tends to be a
lazy type. Male anthropologists delight in telling of societies
in which the men do nothing most of the time except loll
around in hammocks. Otherwise, males specialize in alarms
and excursions. Between long sieges of rest and recovery, the
Kalahari Bushmen of Africa embark on giraffe hunts, hurling
spears to the point of exhaustion in order to bring down one
of these great beasts. Then they strut around it heroically.

The male bands tend to be strongly hierarchical. There
are always chiefs—what Ardrey calls Alpha males—who lend
the group coherence and character. Most men, particularly
when young, have a strong desire to follow and emulate such
leaders. It arises early and continues long. It is the kind of
passion that suggests an instinctive source. And, indeed, it
seems to be part of the pattern that produces the group itself:
leadership, loyalty, and stimulation.

The group is formed and sustained by rites of competition. One wins admission by passing tests, meeting standards, and excelling in contests that embody the values or purposes of the unit. Whether in a hunting party, a military company, a juvenile gang, a football team, or a rock group, membership has value because it is earned. Leadership is revered because it epitomizes the same values. Thus bonding, hierarchy, excellence, and excitement are all assured in the process by which boys and young men gain entry. In fact, it is the process by which they become men as well.

The desire of young men to compete is as profound and insistent as all the other motives and impulses given shape by the bond. All the bonding processes are enjoyed in themselves. It is the contest, the chase, the adventure, the speculation, the risk that enthralls, not the purpose or the goal. This is true even of relatively individual and sedentary scientific ventures, such as the pursuit of the secret of the genetic code. As James D. Watson, co-discoverer of DNA, describes it, it was not the goal but the contest, not the solution but the perplexity, that obsessed the minds and spirits of these colleagues and competitors for so long.[4]

In group efforts of all kinds, this reality is still more salient. The men are gratified to compete and to belong, to lead and to follow—to meet one another and the challenge. Most of the time, they couldn't care less what the ultimate purpose is, as long as society says it is important. That is why any organization or enterprise that offers group fulfillment to young men will release great energies, whether it is a team, a political club, a military venture, a peace demonstration, a motorcycle gang, a criminal conspiracy, religious movement, or a revolution. Wise societies provide ample means for young men to affirm themselves without afflicting others.

Single men can thrive in societies that emphasize male groups of this kind. Often they die, for aggression and combat are perilous. But in most places, through most of human history, life has been short for everyone and the male band has enjoyed some of its more coveted joys: gratifications as primordial and intense in some ways as those afforded by the other crucial human connection, the one between mother and child.

Sexual relations between men and women in most primitive societies were a more episodic and casual affair. The real business of life was among the men, and among the mothers and children. This pattern continued through the Middle Ages in much of Europe. While millions of young single men were engaged in a succession of wars and crusades, banditry and pillage, single women entered one of the multifarious religious orders of the day, joined one of the many all-female guilds, or served the most powerful men and women. The women did much of the community's most essential work. But the single men, as defenders and protectors, could feel important and manly. And because young men were often strongest and most daring, most committed to the group, most entranced by leadership and high rhetoric, they could at least hope to become heroes. But life was grim and short. Women died in labor, men died in battle, millions died in plagues. One prayed for better in the world to come.

That, through much of our evolutionary history, has been the condition of human life. Love and marriage occurred, but rarely together. The emotional ties between men and women that play a central part in civilized human life have been rudimentary and uncoordinated in most human societies. Most rudimentary of all has often been the role of the father. Some one third of all human groups anthropologically recorded are matrilineal—with names and inheritance transmitted through women and with fatherhood a limited and occasional idea. In a quarter of all societies, the man is only a rare visitor to his children.[5] In some tribes, the most famous being the Trobriand Islanders studied by Bronislaw Malinowski, paternity is not even acknowledged. In all such societies, manhood was achieved through group activities with men. In a sense, *all men were single.* Humanity did not reach particularly exalted levels under these circumstances, but at least the men were kept out of the way of the women, who held the major responsibilities for social survival and human progress.

Much has changed today. Today, few men are single. The central bond is not between men, or even between women and children—so we are told to believe. The central bond, the paramount institution, the test of manhood, the fulfillment of life, is the sexual bond between men and women.[6]

There are many reasons for this change. The erratic and short-term rhythms of the battle and the hunt clash with the spirit of modern enterprise. A life that often used to proceed from youth to death through a gauntlet of temporary battles, rituals, and ruttings now is engaged in longer undertakings, investments, and promises: gratifications are foregone, temptations denied, conflicts negotiated. Life passes through seasons and phases and stages, in accord with a rhythm of continuity and growth. It is the way, in fact, life has always been for women, whenever they could arrange it.

Women have always had a concern for the future, a desire for stability, a suspicion of conflict, a skepticism toward the group. They bore the children, vulnerable at the beginning, but full of potentiality. Pregnancy, labor, lactation, and nurture bear the crucial lessons of a life that evolves in time, becoming ever more complex and rewarding. These are the lessons of vulnerability, patience, suffering, and maturity that often render the fitful agitations of men a distraction and a curse.

So the women won, more or less, and therefore society won as well. The all-male group was dislodged from its dominant place in the lives of men. The realm of sexuality, which is the domain of women, supplanted it. This was a crucial step in the evolution of civilized human society. But under modern industrial conditions, this system works best when monogamy is essentially preserved.

In modern life, extended and seasonal, the old male group has moved to the fringes and made the single man the peripheral man. In modern society, only a few men are single beyond their early twenties. They are often failures. Their failure, moreover, is the deepest and most undeniable that one can incur, for it is not some arbitrary cultural lapse, some mercenary shortfall. As human society has now inexorably evolved, singleness discloses a fundamental biological and social inadequacy. Whether consciously or not, most men sense today that they were born to provide support and protection for a woman. Their failure to marry signifies inadequacy in the most definitive masculine terms.

The human race met the challenge of transition from hunting to agriculture and from agriculture to industry in part by shifting the male pursuit from game to women. Through the wombs of women, men can partake in the future of the race. But the hunter in man did not expire; it transpired into higher and more extended endeavors. In the process, society became strongly dependent on the institutions by which the hunter is domesticated—chiefly now the institution of marriage. In general, across the range of modern life, marriage became indispensable to socializing males.

When we speak of the mind and body of the single man, we speak of a mind and body that evolved in all-male groups engaged in the episodic rhythms of hunting and defense. We speak of a mind and body of rudimentary and erratic sexuality, in which fatherhood is but a frail impulse. We speak of a desire to compete, to be tested, to be validated as a man, in a society where manhood was won in the company of men. We speak of a fear and incomprehension of age, which was a rare attainment of evolving mankind. We speak of a rudimentary but intense desire for love and immortality—and that was the way out, for by offering familial roles it could resolve the crises of manhood, of meaning, and of age. But it is hard for the single man to consummate.

A Man and His Body

It is hard to civilize, to change
The usual order;
And the young, who are always the same, endlessly
Rehearse the fate of Achilles.
—LOUIS SIMPSON

Anyone who writes a popular book on sex, or even a violently unpopular one, is apt to find himself on tour. Around the country he goes—from T.V. show to radio studio, from the Morning News to the Midnight Hour, and on into insomnia salvage—listening to his words go forth on the breezes to compete with the stars (or the droning of the late, late show next door).

It is a challenging, frustrating, interesting, and trying circuit. Perhaps most challenging, frustrating, interesting, and trying is the experience of meeting, in every city, a particular woman. She is usually connected to a University, a Mental Health Clinic, an Institute of Sex Research, or a Sex Education group (SIECUS). She is a Professor or a Psychologist or a Lawyer or a Writer. She is stylishly dressed. Normally, she is middle-aged and her introduction reveals a long and scholarly career. Often she is married with several children. She has been there and back, as it were. Nearly every city has one. She is the municipal sexpert.

Her credentials are strong. Perhaps, you imagine, she

will say something interesting or provocative to break the tedium of your own voice, which sounds the same and offers the same opinions in Boston, Detroit, Seattle, and Toronto as it does in New York, Washington, San Francisco, and Los Angeles. Perhaps in the course of her consultations, readings, researches, and experiences, she has developed a theory, or produced a novel idea, or, like the sex therapists, conducted a specific experiment. Perhaps she has some strong personal feelings or arguments.

Well, perhaps. Perhaps the elm tree will be laden with bananas, a Republican will win in the District of Columbia, and taxes will fall. Perhaps, as one sexpert suggested in a rare moment of originality, men's breasts will swell with milk. We don't know. But it isn't very likely.

To begin with, our sexpert will not be available alone. One always finds oneself debating an institution or an academy—some large and august, first-personage plural—the learning of which looms up behind the speaker like a convocation of eminent ghosts, for which she is only a modest medium.

This would not matter necessarily. Her views are more significant if widely and prestigiously held. But what has this Delphic corporation learned about sex? Ask it any question and the answer is the same: "We don't know this"; "We have no evidence for that"; "Our experiments are inconclusive"; "Our knowledge is limited"; "We just don't know." In fact, if one presented in one place all the expressed opinions of these collective experts, one might suppose they were discussing some great mystery—the nature of God, perhaps—and one would have to conclude that it transcended the experience of mankind. More specifically, one would have to conclude that all the "available data" from the "most knowledgeable sources" and most learned authorities, commanding all the "best experimental evidence," had as yet failed to substantiate widely heard rumors and superstitions concerning the existence of "sex." To be sure, *something* is going on out there,

but as to what it is exactly . . . well, "we have very conflicting data on that point. We need more research."

Now only the most extraordinary of individuals could
live for more than thirty-five years and handsomely reproduce
herself, and become a sexpert, without having a clue on the
subject of sex. That is why we have this corporate we, this
agnostic wheeze. Institutes would *not* know anything about
sex. They reproduce by grants and other modes of artificial
insemination. Since Masters and Johnson, most Institutes of
Sex Research have a large interest in perpetuating the idea that
no one knows anything on the subject. It mitigates the otherwise perplexing fact that *they* don't, and they want to assure
their governmental or foundation sponsor that they aren't
onto anything fun—or dirty.

The issue about which "we" are most assuredly and
doggedly agnostic is the existence of two biologically different
sexes. Dr. Babette Blackington, Ph.D., for example, is the
District of Columbia sexpert who alerted me to the unknown
potentialities of male breasts. She finds the whole matter ter-
ribly confusing. "Men's breasts, you know, can be induced to
lactate," she said authoritatively, "and the woman's clitoris
can be made to ejaculate." Although I did not know these
things, I managed to escape the program with my sexist hymen
intact, as it were, and Dr. Blackington departed with her
learned confusions.

The matter of nursing fathers and ejaculating mothers,
however, was too savory to leave in the studio. For it expressed
in vivid terms the ultimate vision of the environmentalist: The
two sexes are essentially identical, inessentially and arbitrarily
divided.

Blackington's source, presumably, was the extended
study of hermaphrodites and other sex anomalies by John
Money and his colleagues at Johns Hopkins University in
Baltimore. If "the sexes are psychosexually neutral" as Money
put it early in his career, in his most quoted opinion, then all
the poetic speculations about hunting parties are interesting

but irrelevant. *Australo-pithecine Africanus* might have been a savage group killer, for various cultural and environmental reasons. But the affluent and technological society of today can create a "new man," a man who can live happily ever after as a sexual nomad or a single housewife, as the needs of the day demand.

It really should be needless to say that this view is wrong, that in a working society the options are limited. For after all these years, scientists are affirming what we have always known: that there are profound and persistent biological differences between the sexes, with which every society must come to terms. As Margaret Mead has written in her great book, *Male and Female:*

> If any human society—large or small, simple or complex, based on the most rudimentary hunting and fishing, or on the whole elaborate interchange of manufactured products—is to survive, it must have a pattern of social life that comes to terms with the differences between the sexes.[1]

What are these differences as they affect the single man? How did the life of the hunter shape his body, his mind, and his social possibilities? Some of the most formidable evidence comes from the studies of Dr. Money himself.[2] Other persuasive material comes from the laboratories of the Harlows at the University of Wisconsin, who have long been examining the habits of Rhesus monkeys.[3] Further evidence comes from studies of baboons, chimpanzees, and other primate cousins, both in captivity and in the wild. Then there are hundreds of interesting experiments with the hormonal systems of rats. Finally, there are scores of experiments and observations among humans from infancy to adulthood, in virtually every kind of society from the most primitive to the most advanced. The evidence, in fact, is so hugely voluminous that our sexperts could be excused for their confusion, if all the material, without important exception, did not point in the same direction: that from conception to maturity, men and women are subjected to different hormonal influences that shape their bodies, brains, and temperaments in different ways.

The man is rendered more aggressive, exploratory, volatile, competitive and dominant, more visual, abstract, and impulsive, more muscular, appetitive, and tall. He is less nurturant, moral, domestic, stable, and peaceful, less auditory, verbal, and sympathetic, less durable, healthy, and dependable, less balanced, and less close to the ground. He is more compulsive sexually and less secure. Within his own sex, he is more inclined to affiliate upwards—toward authority—and less inclined to affiliate downward—toward children and toward the weak and needy.

Of course, these are tendencies that are shaped and transacted by environment and culture, and are modified in crucial ways by the relations between men, women, and children in any society. But most of these propensities are substantiated by a large amount of cross-cultural material, combined with a growing body of physiological, particularly neuro-endocrinological, data.

Among the many interesting cross-cultural comparisons is a study by B. Whiting of six separate cultures—one each in India, Okinawa, the Philippines, Mexico, Kenya, and New England. In all, the boys are more aggressive and violent than the girls and, in all, the girls are more nurturant and responsible—Whiting says dominant—with younger children.[4]

Steven Goldberg, in preparing his fine study, *The Inevitability of Patriarchy*,[5] examined most of the anthropological and sociological literature on the subject of political leadership and authority. In particular, he scrutinized every report of an alleged matriarchy, where women were said to hold political power. He found no evidence that a matriarchy had ever existed or is in any way emerging today. He found no society in which authority was associated chiefly with women in male–female relations. Margaret Mead has described his presentation of the data as "faultless." [6] The degree to which women take power seems to depend on the extent to which the men are absent.

Clelland S. Ford and Frank A. Beach compared sexual patterns in 190 different societies. They found that men are overwhelmingly more prone to aggressiveness, promiscuity, masturbation, homosexuality, voyeurism, sexual attack, and other unstable and indiscriminate sexual activity.[7] George Murdock compared some 500 cultures and found that in all, fighting and leadership were associated with the men.[8]

Now there are two essential ways to deal with a pattern so universal. You can go to the thousands of human societies and find ingenious explanations for each incidence of masculinity and femininity. The men provide most of the food, so they dominate. Or they don't provide most of the food, but the women, feeling secure, allow them to dominate. The men are free from child-care responsibilities and can spend time competing for power. The men are off on the hunt for weeks on end, so the women have more opportunity for politics and are really in control. Or the men really have as much responsibility for the children as the women do, so the men create a pattern of dominance from generation to generation.

One can offer a similar catalogue of particular explanations for the other general patterns. One can find as many partial or apparent exceptions as possible. One can show how the general tendencies can be overcome by conditioning under some circumstances—as when a male Rhesus monkey grooms and fosters an infant put in its cage. One can write a lot about gibbons and beavers and golden hamsters and the few other animals that are less dimorphic than man, and in which the female is the same size as the male or larger. One can assemble the various tests that fail to register differences between the sexes in humans. One can design and give new ones. Then, if you wish, you can say, "We just don't know." "The data on these points is very confusing." "We need more research."

It is simpler, however, to consult the existing research and arrive at a biological or physical explanation. The evidence is ample.

The sexes become significantly different, even in the very organization of their brains, during the time in the womb. There the presence or absence of a Y-sex chromosome determines whether the embryo will be a boy or a girl. The fetus with a Y chromosome will develop testicles rather than ovaries. When the fetus develops male gonads, they will secrete small amounts of androgenic (from *andro*—male, and *genic* —creating) hormones, chiefly testosterone. The testosterone eventually acts on the brain, giving it a male form. So far, neuro-endocrinologists have shown that the hypothalamus is measurably dimorphic, with different weight and cell structure between the two sexes. The hypothalamus is the part of the brain that governs such emotions as hunger, anger, and sex drive. In the man, it also ultimately controls the secretion of the androgens, chiefly testosterone, which themselves have a deep relationship with aggression and sexuality.

The female hypothalamus administers a more complex hormonal system, involving two major sex hormones, estrogen and progesterone, rather than essentially one, as in the male. It also ultimately governs the hormones involved in breast feeding, both in causing lactation (prolactin), creating a desire to nurse, and stimulating the flow of the milk (oxytocin). Oxytocin is also a tranquilizing hormone that encourages nurturant behavior.

The male neuro-endocrinological system—chiefly the hypothalamus and the gonads—is thus less various and flexible than the woman's. The chief male hormone, testosterone, is very powerful and small amounts of it given to a woman greatly stimulate her sex drive (her natural libido hormone is an androgen produced in the adrenal glands). But testosterone is almost the man's whole repertory, the only way he can respond hormonally to a sexual stimulus.

In a sense, sexual inequality begins in the fetus. The

basic human form (template) is female. Even a male fetus will become a healthy *female* if, for some reason, the gonads do not secrete sufficient testosterone in the womb. The fetus becomes male only when it both has a Y-chromosome and is acted upon by androgenic hormones. On the other hand, androgenic hormones cannot make a healthy male out of a female fetus, a fetus with X-chromosomes. But the androgens can cause dramatic virilizing effects. By studying such accidents, one can learn much about the influence of the different hormonal and hypothalamic forms of males and females.

A hormonal accident or malfunction in the womb may cause a later sex confusion, or even a hermaphrodite, with the organs of both sexes. If one has a child of ambiguous sex, one may take it to the clinic conducted in Baltimore by Dr. Money and his colleagues. They have been treating and examining such patients for some two decades and have become the world's leading authorities on the subject.

Many of their findings are presented in a book by Dr. Money and Anke Ehrhardt, called *Man and Woman, Boy and Girl.*[9] Described by *The New York Times* as the most important study published in the social sciences since the Kinsey reports, it is a fascinating exploration of the causes of sexual dimorphism or of its failure to occur.

In order to judge the impact of fetal masculinization on men, it is useful to appraise its effect on the female. Thus we can distinguish to some extent the impact of fetal testosterone on the brain from the continuing influence of testosterone secretions after birth.

There are two principal ways genetic females become androgenized (masculinized) in the womb. One was a medical mistake made in the 1950s—the treatment of pregnant mothers with synthetic progesterone to prevent miscarriage; the substance used contained a hidden androgen. The female fetus absorbed the male hormone. The other way female fetuses become virilized is through a rare and complicated hereditary problem in the adrenal glands. The result is that the fetus secretes extra androgens. In extreme cases of either type, the girl will have an enlarged clitoris like the one Dr. Blackington described. In milder cases, the masculinization is much less visible.

Money and Ehrhardt compared a group of fetally androgenized girls with a group of girls suffering from Turner's syndrome. Turner's girls lack one X-chromosome, making them XO rather than XX. As a result, they lack gonads (ovaries), and produce no sex hormones at all. However, they develop female brains and genitalia, internal and external, and may seem normal until puberty, when they fail to menstruate.

Money and Ehrhardt, therefore, were comparing girls androgenized in the uterus with girls without sex hormones. Both groups were raised as females and identified themselves as such. The results are summarized succinctly by Corinne Hutt, an experimental psychologist at Oxford, in her *Males and Females,* which is the most readable and easily available book on the biology of sex differences: [10]

> Whereas none of the patients with Turner's syndrome showed "intense outdoor physical and athletic interests," all but one of the androgenized females did so; whereas none of the Turner cases regarded themselves or were considered by others to be a tomboy, most of the [androgenized] cases did, and were also regarded so by others. The majority of the androgenized girls preferred boys' toys to girls' toys, some of them playing *only* with boys' toys, while all the Turner girls preferred girls' toys to boys'. The same was true of clothes . . .[11]

On a Draw-a-Person Test, "every one of the Turner's females depicted their own sex first, while only 64 percent of the others did so."

Perhaps the most remarkable result, however, was the apparent influence of fetal experience on carreer and marriage priorities.

No androgenized girls put marriage before a career, some
put a career before marriage and many wanted both; of the
girls with Turner's syndrome, some put marriage before
career, more wanted both, but only one put a career before
marriage and she wanted to be a nun.[12]

One has to understand that these are all cases of considerable abnormality. For all their femininity, the Turner's
girls cannot have children. And unless the severely androgenized girls are found and treated with the appropriate hormones, their voices lower, they develop facial hair, and they
fail to menstruate or acquire breasts at puberty. In cases
where the clitoris is sufficiently enlarged, they can live satis-
factory lives as men, even though they are still internally
female, with ovaries, fallopian tubes, and the upper part of
a vagina.

The point is that these genetic girls can develop a fully
masculine childhood pattern as a result of fetal experience
alone. They still consider themselves girls. But they consistently reject most of the attempts of the culture to feminize
them. One might plausibly conclude, therefore, that the similar
biases in boys, massively reinforced at puberty, are not cultural
fictions. In other words, boys are more aggressive, career-
oriented, and physically exploratory chiefly because of the way
they are born, not the way they are raised. Their brains are
fetally masculinized. The major impact is on the hypothalamus as the center of appetites and emotion, and the thalamus,
which controls the erection, but some experts believe that the
cortex is affected as well.

Many studies of small children indicate that the chief
effect of masculinization is more roughhousing, aggressiveness,
and competition, together with a tendency to affiliate upward,
toward male leaders. The Harlows have demonstrated that, in
monkeys, these effects are slightly diminished rather than
heightened by maternal influence. Male monkeys raised in
cages and fed artificially by simulated cloth "mothers" are

more aggressive with their peers than normal monkeys (while females show just as much feminine "grooming" activity as normal monkeys and vastly more than the males).[13]

It is at puberty that the major hormonal crisis occurs in the lives of boys. Although they are not at that time significantly larger than girls, their bodies begin secreting testosterone in enormous quantities, ten times the androgens received by girls. This has several effects beyond the obvious changes in external sexual characteristics. Testosterone promotes protein synthesis and thus greatly increases physical strength. By fifteen, the boys have shot ahead of the girls in all indices of athletic ability involving muscular strength, height, speed, and cardio-respiratory capacity. Testosterone vastly boosts sexual drive, to the extent that boys reach a peak at age sixteen or seventeen; such "peaking" doesn't happen to women. And, finally, testosterone fosters aggression and competition. Although the precise way testosterone works remains open to question, tests both on humans and monkeys have linked levels of testosterone secretion with levels of aggressive or dominant behavior. And recently scientists have succeeded in changing the dominance order in groups of monkeys by injecting testosterone in the lower-ranking males.[14]

This relationship between testosterone secretion and competitive behavior does not seem to apply in humans much after age thirty. At that point, testosterone secretions—like estrogen flows in women—promote a sense of well-being. At all ages, situations of strain or unhappiness cause the level to drop.

The ability of older men to "hold their hormones," however, does not help the young man. He is full of both aggression and sexual appetite. He wants to join with older boys and participate in highly charged group activity. He wants to define and fulfill his male sex drive. He is swept from day to day by waves of glandular emotion. The theorists of immaculate evolution, who suppose that "the cortex has liberated men from hormonal influence," could not have much observed the behavior of young men.

It is not the exalted cortex that impels their passion for acceptance by the group, their eagerness to compete for a place, their obsessiveness in practicing for the test. It is not cool passages of reason that govern the adolescent's sexual fears and compulsions—his pornographic curiosities, his masturbatory sieges, his ambivalent pursuit of girls. The boy is encountering in acute form the predicament of male sexual identity: a powerful group of drives that lack a specific shape or clear, ultimate resolution in modern society.

The adolescent girl, meanwhile, is often lethargic. Her hormonal surge may depress her. Her body is changing rapidly in ways that are initially uncomfortable. She is entering "the awkward age." But as her body fills out and she becomes a woman, a clear and important sexual role unfolds. Her breasts, her womb, her temperament—together with the increasing interest of boys—remind her of her possible future as wife and mother.

It is an identity of obvious importance to the society. It offers a variety of sensual rewards, from orgasmic sexual fulfillment to childbirth and on into the deep affirmations of breastfeeding and nurture. It is a sexual role that gives a nearly irrevocable value: one's own child. Needless to say, there are also conflicts and complications. Moreover, sexual identity in itself does not resolve all identity problems. But it is an indispensable beginning: a beginning directly related in women to specific and intelligible changes in their bodies and their lives.

It is hard to exaggerate how different is the adolescent boy's experience. His body is not evolving; it is launching an insurrection. It demands to be satisfied now, by external activity. Even in women and in male homosexuals, the injection of testosterone creates a desire for immediate but undefined sexual action.

The most obvious relief, masturbation, is a flight from sexual identity rather than an affirmation of it. Relations with girls, moreover, are ambiguous and complicated at this stage. Rejection of the overwrought male by the underripe female is frequent and deepens the boy's anxieties.

A sexual identity has to involve a role. In the past, there was a direct tie between the boy's growing strength and aggressiveness and his entry into adult male groups. In fact, he might be stronger and faster, a better hunter, than his elders. Like a woman's sexuality, his purpose in life was defined and fulfilled through the changes in his mind and body.

Patricia Cayo Sexton has argued that the relationship between virility and adult acceptance tends to be negative in today's society. Not only do strength and aggression fail to provide a future, they are also likely to jeopardize one's present. She presents voluminous testing data that indicate "feminized" boys do best in school, while the strongest and most aggressive drop out.[15]

Despite all the blather to the contrary, it is obvious that virile men remain attractive to women. They can gain some sense of identity through sex and sports. The chief social problems are created by men of insecure sexual identity who cannot either find girls or excel them in "feminized" school and career competitions. Tests among prisoners indicate that it is the ones with the greatest sexual role anxieties who commit violent and predatory crimes.[16] These are the peripheral males, almost always single, who retaliate against a feminized society for its failure to make them men.

A man who cannot attain his manhood through an affirmative role resorts to the lowest terms of masculinity. What can he do that is exclusively male? He consults his body. He has a cock. But he is a failure and no woman wants it. He has greater physical strength and aggressiveness. He uses it.

The social and hormonal dilemma of young men was illuminated recently by a series of new experiments with Rhesus monkeys in Atlanta.[17] The researchers found that when male monkeys compete, their testosterone levels rise. But when the contest is over, only the winner's remains high. He feels confident, dominant, and ready to pursue females. The loser, on the other hand, is dejected, and his hormone level plummets.

In modern society, sexual relations with women are becoming the chief way a man asserts his sexual identity. But in most of the world's societies, sexual relations follow achievement of manhood, or accompany it. Male affirmation may lead to high testosterone levels, and to feelings of worth, that in turn lead to sexual fulfillment. In this society, it is very hard for many youths to qualify for the company of men on the job or elsewhere. They must validate themselves in sexual terms alone. Yet they lack the confidence and spirit to approach and win a woman.

Ford and Beach's study of more than 190 societies concluded that in virtually all of them sex is regarded as something the woman does for the man.[18] He needs it more urgently than she does. He has no alternative or extended sexual role.

Therefore in every human society the man has to bring something to the woman. He has to perform a service or give a gift. At the very least, he must offer more than his own urgency or he will not even be able to gratify the woman sexually.

Even when he cannot be the provider much of the time, he offers his success as a man, validated in a world of men inaccessible to her. Now, however, the man all too often comes to the woman seeking the very affirmation that he needs to have already if he is to win her. Nothing has occurred in the biology of love that significantly relieves him of this dilemma. The man still has to perform—still has to offer something beyond himself, and beyond her reach—if she is to receive him. Where can he find it?

Rights of the Knife

And therefore—since I cannot prove a lover
To entertain these fair well-spoken days—
I am determined to prove a villain,
And hate the idle pleasures of these days.
Plots have I laid, inductions dangerous,
By drunken prophecies, libels and dreams.
—RICHARD III

The American "incursion" into Cambodia in May 1970 brought to Washington an invasion of protesters. It occurs to me now that in both Washington and Cambodia the bulk of the influx was single men, engaged in characteristic single male activity. The men in Washington were a little richer than the ones marching into Cambodia. But the men in Cambodia were tougher—less guilt-ridden and self-righteous. They also completed their mission, whatever it was, and withdrew to another country.

The Washington group had no other country to which to withdraw. And the specific men with whom I am most familiar—because they occupied my apartment—might well have been happier in Cambodia.

At the time of these "invasions" I was serving as a spokesman for a liberal Republican Senator, Charles McC. Mathias of Maryland. He opposed the incursion but supported the President, and was trying to work something out. This stance put me at a disadvantage in my role of meeting with protesters, who besieged the Senate offices. In their view, I might be against the war, but I was part of the "system." I was left in a morally exposed position. I was also, in a sense, physically exposed. I lived in a basement apartment on Capitol Hill, directly behind the Supreme Court and in the path of demonstrators overflowing the hill.

When I returned from my office the evening before the demonstration, my need for moral support created an uneasiness that reached beyond the dilemmas of my job. I also had qualms about my virility. Not only was I avoiding enemy fire in Southeast Asia, I was also shunning full commitment in Washington. Thousands of young men and women would be marching the next day full of moral fervor, while I would be worrying about violence, about affronting powerful Senators who might vote for peace.

In a way, I knew my commitment was deeper, more practical, professional. But it didn't allow a fusion of physical and emotional engagement: a delivery of myself to the group and the cause.

Under the circumstances, it seemed, the only thing I could do was run. Running had served me well ever since my days in competitive track. A good run could give me a sense of manliness and moral sufficiency often lasting several hours —perhaps long enough to get me to sleep. I would need sleep to face the next day.

So off I went on my run, striding past the Supreme Court, around the Capitol, down the Mall to the Washington Monument, through clots of protesters and guardsmen, down along the reflecting pool to the Lincoln Memorial, running loose and strong and free, out toward Hains Point, savoring the scent of blossoms in the deepening dusk, past groups of returning fishermen, couples in the grass, sweeping by a pair of joggers, feeling the cool spring breezes and the warm wash of sweat on my chest, and having the sense of being a man at one with his body and the world.

Then I did the turn and headed back on the other side of the Point, working harder now, fighting for breath, feeling the muscles more—no fluid speed and grace—but sure of the strength and the will to return, sure even of a kick at the end up Capitol Hill, past the guardsmen and protesters—would they remember and marvel?—past the glowing marble office buildings, pumping along the sidewalk, struggling on up to the Supreme Court—the heart, the legs beating together, beating hard against the stiffness and pain and pavement, until, at last . . . all smooths and froths for the final sprint, the accustomed miracle—and I would fall on the lawn in front of my apartment. How many of the invaders, or incursors, could do that number? I thought.

But I hadn't done it yet. I had the final miles up by the monuments and the Capitol still to go, and still to come was my redemptive clash with the National Guard.

It happened as I labored, gasping for air, up the hill by the Washington Monument. I heard something drop in front of me.

I ignored it . . . then was bowled to the ground in the darkness, as if by a bullet in the gut or a noose at the neck. For a moment I was doubled over, unknowing and terrified. Then I realized it was some kind of tear gas.

Whoever thought of using tear gas against demonstrators was a genius. It provides a perfect atmosphere for virility games.

The next day, for example, a large group of protesters decided to attack John Mitchell's Justice Department. Some of them allegedy managed to hoist a Vietcong flag up one of the flagpoles. I didn't see it, and there were no photographs available, so I don't know. But I have a clear image of how they launched the attacks that reminded John Mitchell of the Russian Revolution—and me of two-handed touch in the park.

They would huddle together in small bands, dressed in old sweatshirts and army fatigues, looking like groups of sandlot football players—except grimmer by far, for this was a game of combat and lives were at stake. The quarterback would mutter directions. Then they would break out with a yell and charge toward the police lines on Pennsylvania Avenue.

But, alas, there are casualties, nearly 100 percent; the whole squad is on the pavement clutching at their faces. They are twisted in mortal pain. A girl rushes forward with wet towels and handkerchiefs. Will they live? Yes. They get up and straggle back, cursing under their breath. They know there is nothing Washington won't do to stop them now (short of actual bodily harm).

"We got to go again," one of them mutters.

"Not right away?"

"Yeah," he says, "We got no choice." (The pigs might leave.)

So back in the huddle the wounded gather, and back they charge to Pennsylvania Avenue, where they once again can feel the sweet agony of war—and survive. For a time, at least, they could escape their fatal awareness that the older generation had been *tested* in combat and had met the test, while the young rebels had not even faced the draft. The older men had undergone the primordial rites of the warrior. Perhaps they were the last true warrior generation of Americans. The young rebels had failed even to find a testing ground and were reduced to an imitation of the old. Groping for manhood, they drank tear gas the way some men drink whiskey, to feel strong and avoid the truth. At least it was better than heroin, or Vietnam.

Back on the hill the night before, I had gradually become aware of what had happened to me and was enraged. Then, within five minutes, the pain miraculously lifted and I could see. Along the mall, lit by street lamps, were clusters of helmeted police, National Guardsmen, tourists, demonstrators. Floodlights occasionally swept the scene, sirens screamed in the dark, proclaiming the urgency of the moment. It was pregnant with history, I thought. But falsely pregnant, I think now, a fever of memory in the night. The rites of manhood will no longer be dignified by history. History is now made by leaders and their incomprehensible machines. Instead, there will be sieges of hysteria as each generation of young men rises to the false occasions of their passage to an unknown—would it be an androgynous?—world.

And part of the hysterical pregnancy of that moment was Vietnam itself. Was that lingering, suppurating war a part of history, part of a larger evolution of great events, transcending the squalid present? I hope not, for it would likely be a pattern of national decline. Was it not rather a tragically blind repetition of the rites of passage that defined manhood for the older generations?

As I stood there on the hill, however, recovering from the gas, I was not exactly pensive or philosophical. I was surprised by a surge of elation. It might not be history but it had made me part of the flow of events. I saw that I must have been one of the very first demonstration casualties. Perhaps *the* first. As each group of protesters came into the Senator's office the next day, I could score an immediate connection—even a point of vantage. Only tear gas could have done that, inflicted such intense and total and yet transitory pain—created so profound and yet so harmless a baptism by fire.

I ran up to my apartment, sprinting the last quarter mile, and headed across the street to my little plot of grass. But there were people already there, four demonstrators, three boys and a girl, smoking cigarettes and drinking beer. My rage at the tear gas returned. But then it occurred to me that here was an audience for my story. I certainly needed an audience. In fact, I would have had to go out and find one if this group had not already assembled. And then, too, I saw that they were comrades.

In the spirit of the moment, I invited them to stay the night. Three of them remained for nearly a month. I was in my last weeks on the Hill before returning to Cambridge and was speaking to an average of six or seven groups a day, as well as writing speeches. I was very busy. I can think of other reasons why I didn't kick them out. Perhaps I am generous. But I think the real reason was that I was reluctant to confront them. One of them, you see, was Louie.

Louie was one of the leaders of the assault on the Justice Department. He was not typical of them; I knew some of the others. But he was sure to be in the middle—sure to rise to the top—and sure to be the one who slugged the cop at the end. He was released two days later in the "custody" of a friend, another of my guests.

On the first evening, Louie did not strike me as greatly different from the others. He was older—in his early twenties —more glib, issuing long spiels about "fascism" and "pigs" and "revolution." But he was also more ingratiating, with his shock of black hair, his glittering eyes, his warm smile, his sexual magnetism. He knew how to talk to me. He would tell me, "I mean, I really dig what you're doin'. We got to have guys on the inside, man. Everybody's got to work together, get it together. I *dig* that." That night, after my collision with the gas, I was ready to get it together with Louie. I gave them all dinner and promised to go down and watch them take over Justice the next afternoon.

Except for glimpses through the smog on Pennsylvania Avenue, I did not see Louie again for three days. I was sitting in my apartment, writing a speech at three a.m. I had taken for granted that the group had left, and the loud knock on the door startled me. Unshaven and disheveled, at first they did not even look familiar through the peephole. I let them in hesitantly. I had work to do, I said, and it would be be better if they went somewhere else. "Sure, man," Louie said, "all we want is somethin' to eat." I nodded toward the kitchen and they piled into the icebox, gulping down quarts of milk, chomping at bars of cheddar cheese, devouring salami, dried apricots, ginger ale, ice cream; everything but my yoghurt was consumed, while I sat trying to compose an eloquent

statement for the Senator on why the United States should
ratify the U.N. "Genocide Convention," when the only good
argument was "why not?"

Louie then walked over to the desk and gave me a pen.
I looked at it with annoyance and started to give it back.

"No, it's for you. I'm givin' it to you," he said. There
was something in his face I had not seen before, a note of
menace: when Louie gives you something, you take it. I
picked it up. It was handsomely designed but did not fit com-
fortably in my hand; it was too heavy. "Gee, thanks," I said,
"but I really have to get back to work."

"Press the button," he said. "Press it. It's on the top."

I looked at the pen and started trying to take off the
top. He leaped across the room and ripped it from me.

"Jesus, man, you'll cut yourself to pieces that way. We
can't have you dyin' on us." He laughed loudly.

"Look," he said. He lifted the pen in his right fist, held
it up so the biceps of his arm bulged, and pressed the top with
his thumb. A stiletto glittered in his hand. He stepped forward.
His face was hard. Then it dissolved into a sweet smile. "Here,
it's yours," he said. "It's worth fifty dollars."

I thanked him again, too effusively, and tried to address
the matter of genocide. My guests moved into the next room
and started thumbing through my record collection. They
chose the Rolling Stones, loudly.

When I returned from the office the next night at eleven,
they were still there, the Stones were still struggling to get
satisfaction, there was another girl, and marijuana smoke
was heavy in the air. That did it. "Jesus, I can't have this," I
said, "you guys get busted and nothing much happens, maybe.
I get busted and I lose my job and any hope of getting another
one. I'm through."

"All right, man, cool it," Louie said.

But I was still hot. "You know how many fucking cops
pass this house every day? Every hour?"

"He's right," said one of the others.

"You know what that building is across the street?" I asked. "That is the fucking Supreme fucking *Court* of the United States. You guys talk about the pigs. Man, you're right in the middle of the sty, right now, right on the fuckin' top of Porkchop Hill."

"He's right," Louie said, "put out the joint."

I walked into the kitchen to get some food. There was an opened can of V-8 juice and some discolored cheddar cheese remaining. They had acquired a taste for yoghurt.

I was about to go back and protest. But Louie had followed me in and put his hand on my shoulder. "We really appreciate what you're doin' for us. That joint was stupid. Sometimes I just don't think too good." I said it was all right. I understood. I said I was sorry I had lost my temper. "Forget it, man," he said, "nobody's perfect."

A few days later, I moved in with a girl on the other side of town. I really had been planning to do it for some time. But before I did, I received a lesson in astrology. It was the first and only time I had ever talked about astrology for more than five minutes with anyone whom I was not in the process of seducing. Louie had a way about him that made you listen.

"What's your sign?" he asked me.

"I don't know," I said. It was a conceit of mine not to know my sign.

"Jesus, man, no bullshit, what's your fuckin' sign?" he asked. I looked blankly back. "Well, when the hell were you born?"

"November 29, 1939."

"What time?"

"How am I supposed to know that?" I asked. I really didn't want to continue the conversation. "Look, I got to get some stuff together. I'm going to be staying with this girl for a few days. And I wish you guys . . ."

He took out a knife like the one he had given me and flipped it into the table top. Later I found it was the one he had given me. I ignored it.

"I wish you guys could find some other place," I said. "I don't want to kick you out, but . . ."

"Yeah, man, I dig you," he said, then hesitated. "But tell me. What time was it you were born? Just more or less. If you can give me the time, I can figure out what your stars are. It can really help you out, I'll tell ya." I nodded. He continued. "Like *my* stars. They say I will have a life of sex and violence." He looked pensively at the knife and put it back in his pocket. "It's really helped me to know that," he said.

I didn't ask him how, so I am still not exactly clear on what he meant. But I didn't try to kick them out before moving. I guess in a way they kicked me out. When I returned a week later, all my records were gone, together with my record player and my food. But in exchange they had left several fish in my icebox—the type you get from the Potomac out on Hains Point. They were not cleaned and their odor suffused the kitchen. There was also a girl in my bed.

I had not noticed her much during the previous weeks. I was seldom in the apartment and Louie was the one who did most of the talking. She was a short, moderately pretty blonde girl, with a sullen, usable look, and few words. She had slept with Louie. I assumed she was an old friend, but it turned out they had met on my lawn the night of the demonstration.

She had come down from New York, she said. The others were from Pittsburgh. She had no idea where they had gone, but she understood Louie had found a car. She was indignant that they had taken the record player. She said she had not had any music for three days. Her name was Mattie. She was fifteen.

I had had enough. I sent her packing with her paper bag full of clothes and told her to go to the YWCA—hesitating only a moment when she said it was all right if we slept in the same bed. I had qualms, though, as I closed the door. I ran after her down the street and gave her a five-dollar bill. She took it happily. Nonetheless, I felt somehow guilty as I walked back to my room. I guess I realized that I was part of the system—Louie's system.

The system of the Louies of the world—and there are millions of them—has nothing to do with the morality of cooperation and negotiation, justice and equality that one likes to think governs human life. Louie combined attraction and power in a way that mesmerized all around him. Alan Harrington wrote a book about this type—*The Psychopaths*[1]—which he defines as completely manipulative and egocentric, lacking conscience or remorse. He believes that their numbers are rapidly increasing in the United States. The most coherent of the many theories considered in his book suggests that these men are in some way disaffiliated: since earliest childhood they have lacked love, lacked connections to family and society. They become independent and amoral.

These men are incapable of loving others. But, strangely enough, they have a great capacity for attracting followers of both sexes. Charles Manson and the Symbionese Army's Daniel DeFreeze are extreme examples. Louie seemed milder but he had similar powers. He readily dominated his group and immediately took the only woman in it. He even managed to disarm and exploit me, an older outsider, a male who was much richer and more "powerful" in conventional terms.

His success, however, will surprise only those who assume that the moral values inhering in family life also prevail easily in the society at large. In our day-to-day lives outside the family, Louie's system—the system of raw power, implicit violence, sexual magnetism, and the potency of leadership—is at least as powerful as the system of law and morality. Above all, Louie's system rules among the unmarried, who are living in the present, without dependents or dependencies, without a stake in the past or future, without children.

The only way to discipline these men, other than through marriage, is through adult male groups. As much as possible the young male predators must be broken and subdued—their aggressions tempered and channeled—by dominant men. This is one of the most important functions of the virility rites and initiations found in nearly every primitive society and lingering in various forms—teams, clubs, and fraternities—even in our own.

We may find we need such devices more than ever. Modern society in its great complexity and interdependence is also gravely vulnerable to the antisocial male: the hijacker, the saboteur, the mugger, the bomber, the "revolutionary." The failure to discipline their male aggressions is deadly to the social order. Schools on prisons cannot do it alone in a democratic system. Across a whole society, only the complex of roles in the family and the male group can integrate men.

A single man, independent and fearless, can terrorize a whole community.

While I write this there is outside, somewhere in the night of this small French island, a robber. He escaped last week from the local jail. So far he has taken some 3,000 dollars' worth of watches from the local department store, several thousand in cash from the airport, and a large amount of jewelry. Each night, he robs some isolated native family of food. Monsieur Salazar, my ex-French army caretaker, is waiting outside in the darkness for him to return here. The last time he came by, Salazar gave chase up the mountain behind the house and nearly caught him. If Salazar had had his dog—a ferocious long-haired German shepherd—the robber would be back in jail now. I am not worried that he will try this place again.

The local gendarme has a problem. The people on the island talk about nothing but *le voleur*. Every day several groups of islanders see him. It is a white population; he is black and easily identifiable. When any of the natives spot him, they run. That is the problem.

But the gendarme does have a plan. He expects that at some point the robber will tire of this island. It is a small place and there is nowhere to sell his watches or spend his money or find nocturnal entertainment. Sooner or later, *le voleur* will steal a boat and leave. The gendarme's plan is to wait until he does. They will deal with him on Saint Martin, he says.

Margaret Mead has written extensively about a small New Guinea tribe called the Mountain Arapesh. They are small because they are not very good at reproducing or feeding themselves and they are the *mountain* Arapesh because the more belligerent tribes in the valleys have driven them ever farther up the barren slopes.[2]

The Arapesh are one of the most humane and attractive of all Mead's groups. They seem to be governed by the kind of social morality that we prefer. Both the men and the women spend much of their time in child-rearing. Let her describe them:

> . . . a mild undernourished people, they are . . . always struggling to save enough to buy music and dance steps and new fashions from the trading peoples of the sea coast, and to buy off the sorcerers among the fiercer people of the interior plains. Responsive and cooperative, they have developed a society in which, while there is never enough to eat, each man spends most of his time helping his neighbor, committed to his neighbor's purposes. The greatest interest of both men and women is growing things—children, pigs, coconut trees—and their greatest fear that each generation will reach maturity shorter in stature than their forebears, until finally there will be no people under the palm trees.[3]

Not only are the Arapesh not a productive society, they are also not a creative one. "The Arapesh," Mead writes, "admire so deeply the artistic products of others that they have developed practically no art of their own." It is a society in which feminine values of nurture and receptivity prevail. But as Mead reports, the men are incapable of giving the women orgasm. It is a society where the greatest value is children but where the children die for lack of food.

It is a society where both sexes are raised in the same way. But "that makes it much more difficult to be a male, especially in all those assertive, creative, productive aspects of life on which the superstructure of a civilization depends."

The men grow up full of guilts and fears. They are terrified of "strange, oversexed women from other tribes who will take part of their semen and use it for sorcery." One Arapesh man described the process to Mead:

> She will hold your cheeks, you will hold her breasts, your skin will tremble, you will sleep together, she will steal part of your bodily fluid; later she will give it to the sorcerer and you will die.[4]

The Arapesh males have elaborate initiation rites. They consist of acts of blood-letting and self-mutilation, as the men imitate the menstruation and child-bearing of the women.

There is a fashionable belief today that masculinity is outmoded. When encountering the warrior mystique, the nomadic rhythm, the hunter's physique, the combatant bond, the sexual compulsion—all the awkward legacies of manhood —computers gag and moan like a convention of N.O.W. The computers have a point. Hunters, warriors, and nomads seem irrelevant in the shadow of the mushroom cloud. The remaining warriors and nomads among us, moreover, create a long series of social problems.

In Studs Terkel's *Working,* a tape-recorded catalogue of workers, the men who are policemen and firemen seem happiest in their calling. But in a democratic society there is still a limited need for policemen. In every military service, the groups assigned to the most perilous work—from paratroopers and fighter pilots to frogmen and Green Berets—display the highest morale. But we do not want John Wayne or Audie Murphy at mission control, not to mention missile control. We do not even need trigger fingers on the button; typing fingers will do all too well. Why not feminize the men? The new society subsists on feminine virtues anyway: Long horizons, a sense of growth, a sense of human sanctity, a commitment to future generations are all more valuable than the primal loyalties and aggressions of the male band.

Yet there is another possibility: A healthy society, in all its millions of private dealings and contests, needs a male principle at work. The streams of our social life need male corpuscles, male bonds, male antibodies, or the residual warriors among us will bully and demoralize us all.

Isn't it possible that part of our current agony as a people derives from the confusion and flight of manhood? Isn't the failure of people to resist the aggressors among us, the failure of the police to arrest the criminal, the failure of the group to condemn the amoral exploiter of other men's women or work more a reflection of a collapse of will than of a blurring of vision? The female principle of moral perception may be healthy. It may even thrive as never before among our youth. But to enforce it, to make it real from day to day, we need men. And it is the ties of male enforcement—of group discipline, supervision, loyalty, and selection—that are failing.

The men, most of them, are connected to women and to moral values, but they are not connected to one another and to the community. Thus they are unwilling to fight for the values they hold. The processes of testing and certification—in our schools, businesses, and bureaucracies, even in our charities and clubs—are being desexed and industrialized. The personal group is being disbanded. The result is that the male–female bond may become overloaded while our larger social connections deteriorate.

From the perspective of computer justice—the justice of neutral units rather than diverse humans—the values of family, kinship, and group loyalty are immoral: The words for them are nepotism and bigotry. But in the deeper, natural morality of the race, these values have their social purposes, and we need to maintain a careful balance. The private club, the family business, the ethnic guild, the church all contribute to the integration of men into a society where connections and responsibilities have sinew and blood, memory and promise—in which the man being attacked in the street is a brother, a cousin, a colleague, a parishioner, a cohort, a member. He is helped. When real ties dissolve, it is not to liberate a sense of justice but to unfetter the exercise of raw power. And single men have the fewest real connections of all.

The debate over the role of aggression in human society has been needlessly roiled and inflamed by the issue of killing. Robert Ardrey's theories and speculations are heavily documented by archeological evidence. His essential point is almost certainly true: The hominid kin of man were carnivorous hunters and they killed their prey before eating it—even most of the time before cooking it. This fact does not seem to me very sensational, unless you wish to believe that men are biologically destined to vegetarianism. Ardrey's theory might raise a further question of human sadism. But while we know humans can be sadistic, we also know that sadism is not our dominant impulse. It is obvious that men kill chiefly in extreme circumstances and that a truly internecine society would have run into serious evolutionary trouble. Killing is only one facet of aggression, found chiefly in war and hunting and in a few tribal initiation rites, but it is not a paramount theme of humanity.

Aggression and bonding play other vital roles in society —roles of moral enforcement, male socialization, protection of women and children, and provision for their needs. They give emotional traction to the dangerous responsibilities of the police and to the continual acts of resistance and constraint, which maintain a social order. They give energy and vitality to the fight for justice and compassion, for the ideals that the society cherishes. In negative terms, the point is expressed in the bumper sticker that says, "Next time you're mugged, will you call a hippy?" But the principle applies everywhere that the various economic and psychic muggings of our time occur. The denial of aggression or the attempt to abolish the impulse in men may well create a more threatening and exploitative society in which the Louies and other psychopaths, from high government offices to the streets, ride roughshod over everyone else.

Steven Goldberg has remarked that natural male aggressiveness today is treated like sex in Victorian England. It is a fact of life that the society largely condemns and tries to suppress and that its intellectuals ignore or deny. It is a physiological and psychological reality that is not acknowledged to have consequences for social policy. We are not allowed to suppose that male aggression will inevitably lead to male dominance in most competitive activities. We assume instead that the successful man is a product of discrimination against women. We fail to recognize that the absence of arenas for aggressive male groups will lead to the eruption of such aggressions against the society itself, or the festering of them in the minds of the men. And as in Victorian England, when suppression of sex led to an epidemic of perversity—all kinds of lurid flowers in the secret gardens of society, so the denial of male affirmation in modern life leads to pervasive distortions and perversions of healthy masculine aggression—to violence and pornography, to fear and exploitation of women, to the quest for potency through drugs and alcohol, to punch-drunk music, and to fighting at sports events. Millions of feckless men feed on the masculinity of a few heroes—boxers, football players, politicians, rock stars.

The result is a society that simultaneously denies the existence of natural male aggressiveness and is continually preoccupied with it. Male aggression and violence animate our movies, T.V. shows, magazines, newspapers, politics, culture. Our city streets are quailed by it. Our city schools are terrorized by it. "Liberated" women are obsessed by it—laboring through hours of karate, palavering endlessly through rap sessions on rape. It would be better to confront the reality and address the real problem, which is the lack of ways for men to achieve sexual identity and express aggression.

"Human identity" alone won't do. Sexual identity derives from experiences and actions that feel distinctively male. Men need a mode of sexual validation that is the counterpart of the female potential for procreation, which is the birthright of almost every woman.

10

Jobs Without Gender

A performer is a person who needs immediate communication and an immediate reward . . . . You're naked when you perform.

—RUBY BRAFF (Jazz trumpeter)

If one wants to know why single men in America often lack long-term relationships with women and affirmative ties to male groups, one need only look at their jobs. Most men spend much of their time at work, and even their activity beyond the workplace greatly depends on how much money they make and whom they meet on the job. In addition, in the modern world, the job is one of the remaining ways that young men are integrated into adult society.

For single men, however, the workplace is often an arena of emasculation and poverty, where they are estranged from women and elders rather than joined with them in a larger moral order. Single men at work fall into two main categories: blue-collar workers, who often get a sense of male identity but little money, and white-collar workers, who usually get neither.

Some of the more manly jobs come around cars and trucks. Down at the service station, most of the time, it is a single man pumping gas. The mechanic in back, with the beer can and *Penthouse,* "tuning up" your engine to the music from the rock station, may well be single too. Many mechanics are skilled professionals who gain a sense of masculine competence in their jobs. The truck driver pulling in is a little older; he is listening to country music; 260,000, about a fifth of them, are bachelors.[1] The truck drivers have created an affirmative male culture of music and slang and camaraderie. They have heavy responsibilities. But their earnings are short.

When Congresswoman Martha Griffiths looks at a truck driver, she sees a man with money: a median income, she guessed resentfully during her Hearings on Discrimination, of 16,000 dollars heading for 25,000.[2] The fact is, truck drivers' median income is a little over 7,000 dollars.[3] Four fifths of them have wives and children.

Another quarter million single men are farm workers. They average about half as much money as the truck drivers. About 40,000 of the farm workers, though, live the nomadic life, get to see the country, get a tan if they need it. But they earn even less than the settled farm worker. Do they know that boys in college sing songs about them?

Few songs are sung about the men in the back rooms, in the semi-darkness and dust, moving stock and freight, pushing dirty clothes into baths of chemicals, cooking other people's hotdogs, washing other people's dishes. But there are over a million of them—a sixth of all working single men —earning a median of 5,000 dollars a year.

In airier places, out front, there are another quarter million—sales clerks; they get to see money chiefly in cash registers. The voyeur kings of single finance, however, are the tellers in the banks. There are 100,000 single male tellers, with a median income of 6,500 dollars.

About a million single men are office functionaries of one sort or another, earning a median income of about 7,500 dollars, which is relatively good for bachelors. But the best job held by large numbers of single men—and twice as many single women—is teacher. There are 240,000 single male teachers with a median income over 9,000 dollars.[4]

That is about it. All the other categories of bachelor workers put together reach only into the hundreds of thousands. For example, there are only a total of 50,000 single male doctors and lawyers, and 140,000 engineers and computer specialists.[5]

In general, if you are not going to pay them well, men are happiest working with other men in challenging and virile activity. At its best, the job can be an important mode of initiation to manhood, and the male group can transmit important values to the young man coming up. Very few of the jobs held by single men in America serve this function.

The jobs of single men correspond closely to the jobs of single women. The women stay out of the trucks and gas stations and construction sites, most of the time; and out of the barns and fields and orchards, some of the time. But they are right there in the stores and banks, schools and offices, restaurants and laundries. Deployed among the hundreds of thousands of single male office clerks are millions of female secretaries and typists trying to avoid them and pursue men at higher levels. Among the hundreds of thousands of short-order cooks and dishwashers are hundreds of thousands of waitresses dodging their hands and eyes. Watch the female tellers ignore the camaraderie of the men and flirt with the officers. Listen to the stewardess talk to Studs Terkel:

"When you first start flying, the men you meet are airport employees: ramp rats, cleaning airplanes and things like that, mechanics . . . we get tired of that, so we move into the city to get involved with men that are usually young executives . . . They wear their hats and their suits and in the winter their black gloves."[6]

Increasingly, though, the young "executives" are surrounded by women competitors too—management trainees, executive secretaries. Their bosses are moving them into the spotlight for the Equal Employment Opportunities Commission. It is not the reassuring luminescence of soft lights at the corner bar, the sultry shadows.

The jobs that single men do with women are often sexually demeaning to the men. The secretary can marry her boss, can bear his children. She can go out with the young executive. Her social and sexual value, though influenced by class, is little affected by her earnings and occupational status. The man's situation is radically different. What he does and how much he makes virtually define his sexual worth—his very manhood. If a man is going to make little money, be humiliated at his job, at the very least he wants to do it in the company of men. All across America today he works among the disdainful faces of women. Should he dare ask one out? You must be kidding. There will be guffaws in the ladies room within the hour.

Where single men and women work at the same jobs, the women are socially superior. They know it and the men know it. The woman's hauteur is answered by the man's sexual contempt, male chauvinism. It makes for an emotional balance, but not for an amicable workplace, affirmative to men. The fact is that whatever are the benefits of a breakdown of sexual roles in employment, better relations between the sexes are not among them. Talk about the need to see women as equals is not very helpful to men who already, in their guts and pocketbooks, experience women as superior. For their protection as men they try to forget, summon old, ugly ideologies. But they do not really believe in them.

One popular answer to the problem—particularly among those who have a lot of material goods—is to move beyond materialism, beyond masculinity. Radical professors, rock singers, multimillionaire troubadours, all tell the single man to forget the games of the office and the marketplace. They tell him that regularity, neatness, toughness, and obedience are square—symbols of submission to an evil or stodgy establishment. They tell him that a concern with money or status is mercenary and contemptible. They tell him that he needs no material advantage over women in order to qualify for marriage and family—and who indeed wants to qualify for that? (Except the radical professors, rock singers, and multi-millionaire troubadours.) He is told to be radical, compassionate, nurturant, and sensitive.

He is not informed, however, that this pattern is almost completely its own reward. You won't even get to sleep with Germaine Greer; she goes for construction workers.[7] Her hankering for the effeminate is a matter of theory. Other feminist women might find you nice for a while. But it will end soon. As the massive survey of male and female attitudes by Anne Steinmann and David Fox (*The Male Dilemma*) has shown, women want "a man even more active, self-oriented, and aggressive than the men were or wanted to be." [8]

The anti-masculine mode damages the single man's sexual possibilities, dims his marital prospects, subverts his hopes for a happy and productive future, and ultimately evokes the disdain of the very women who call for it. The man who accepts the effeminist prescription as more than a rhetorical litany is trampled under the feet of the men and women who instinctively know it is a joke.

One of the sadder sights in America today is the lapsed and wilted flower child. Taught to believe that aggressiveness and competition are evils in themselves and that success is unattractive to women, he ends up on the street without either women or money. He can often be found on the winter circuit of the Revolution, shaking a fist or a tambourine, moving from one fashion in drugs or religion to another. He goes from Salvation Pharmacies to Mobile Home Mosques, from guru entrepreneurs to Zen boodlers, all the while living off friends more provident or lucky than he is. The street religions he chooses have the minimal virtue of being doggedly patriarchal. But for all his acclaimed passivity, all he can talk about, much of the time, is violence. In the end, he is likely to turn it against himself, or against the society.

No program advocated by American liberals or radicals will bring us one iota closer to a less materialistic and competitive society. The emphasis on female job advancement and

Sexual Revolution just makes the contest more sexually and socially invidious. The women professionals marry professional men, not flower children.

In general, the successful woman demands that her man be even more successful than she is. The increasing difficulty of finding such extraordinary creatures means that career girls are marrying later and divorcing more. (The real successes lead the league in divorce.) [9] Thus the demands placed on men, insidiously tacit but inescapable, are greater than ever.

Women insist, as they always must, on the man's continued exertions to remain chief provider, protector, and stud. The modern woman merely offers more readily her own competition and more grudgingly her respect for a special male place and virtue. Even those few women who do permit the man to stint on his material responsibilities require a psychological and sexual confidence on his part that is difficult to achieve without victories of one kind or another in those "status" competitions so disdained by feminists. Only 8 percent of American women say they would respect a man for choosing to stay home and care for children.[10]

Contrary to the claims of the women's movement, these women are not wrong or culpable. They do not have to inflict the system on men, because it is already in men. Men already know that if they are to win a high-status woman for more than a brief sexual entertainment, they had better be high-status themselves. There are few facts of life that men know so well. To find an acceptable woman, a man must perform.

Single men, therefore, are in an awkward position today. They must try to marry women who are making as much money as they are. This puts them at a serious disadvantage, since psychologically and sexually they are less stable, more compulsive, and, in truth, more in need of marriage than the women are. The divorced man is in a similar plight if he is pursuing a young woman.

For young single and divorced men, the problem is that

a young woman wants a potential husband to show an ability to support and protect her and her children. The man instinctively accepts this requirement. It is not a peculiarity of capitalism, but a universal fact of life. As Margaret Mead has observed, and as cross-cultural studies throughout anthropology have shown, the male has to provide for the woman in some way if he is to be a full part of the family.[11]

This demand for a male provider role originates not only in culture but in biology as well. The other male roles in the family are relatively tenuous and dispensable. His part in procreation is small. But, at least when young, his need for sex is more urgent. Therefore, the man has to compensate the woman if he is to benefit from her sexuality, her long pregnancy, labor, and nurture—if he is to partake through her in the future of the race. Although the man is less likely to be the only provider today, the provider role may even have assumed greater importance for men in recent years, since the protector role has been largely surrendered to the police. Few men are exempted from either role. Usually, when the man can no longer support his family, he leaves it. His feelings of inadequacy as a man strike too deeply for logic to assuage.

The single man's problem is thus that he must still prove an ability as provider in a society where he cannot earn more money than most of the females eligible to him. It is a difficult dilemma and it accounts for some of the single male's distresses. Unable to feel needed by women, he attempts to feel superior to them. He moves into the male groups of failure in the bars and on the streets, feeds his vanity with drugs and alcohol, and demeans women. Says he doesn't need 'em or they're all the same in the dark. But he knows it doesn't even really wash down with the liquor.

The fact is that in general a man is sexually and socially crippled by economic failure—doomed to brief and inconsequential relationships—while a woman's sexual prospects are damaged hardly at all. From the ballroom to the bedroom she has always been valued more for what she is than for what she does or how well she performs. Men are always on trial.

This fundamental inequality is not a mere cultural contrivance. It cannot be changed, because it derives from the man's inevitable sexual inferiority. He is optional. One man can impregnate a hundred women, but only one woman can bear a man's child and acknowledge his paternity. Even then the probation continues, since usually, if there is an extreme conflict, the woman can take away the child. It is what the man does, how he performs, what he provides that overcome his biological dispensability.

However fashions may change, therefore, women will seek strength and performance in men; they want providers and protectors for themselves and their children. Any propaganda to the contrary can be safely ignored as the issue of hopeful failures and defensive successes. Men and women already on the heights are glad to tell the competitors gathering below that one can find the universe in a joint of grass.

The need to perform is not only a deep social fact of male existence. It is also a sexual fact, dramatized in the act of love. The man must be potent and commanding if intercourse is to succeed. He is on stage, naked, before his judge. No matter how he postures at the bar, or among the boys, the test that matters is in the bedroom, and the performance that counts is his own.

In women's literature, as in men's, there is a lot of talk about whether women are "good in bed." This, I believe, is a projection of men, designed to relieve their own anxieties. It is the men who succeed or fail in sexual performance. A woman may be more or less beautiful, more or less loving. But she cannot really fail like an impotent or premature man. From the man's point of view, it does not matter much what she *does* in bed as long as she does not try to take over inopportunely and as long as she expresses the feeling that she desires the man. The man is the one who is tested—tested again and again.

The essence of the passage to manhood, in fact, is a series of trials. Young single men now may pass or fail the sexual test at an early age. They continue to bear the provider burden. And their manhood among men is also a matter of performance. The boy applying to the older group is not admitted, most of the time, for his good looks. He must play well in the game; he must shoot straight; he must fight hard; he must know his musical chops. He must show he is a worthy competitor and performer.

This pattern obtains in our society and in every other. It is not really optional. The diffuse energies and compulsions of the teenaged boy must be shaped into the constructive activities of manhood. As Margaret Mead has written, "The worry that boys will not grow up to be men is much more widespread than that girls will not grow up to be women, and in none of the South Sea societies does this latter fear appear at all." [12] The girls evolve into women; the boys evolve into vessels of disruptive energy. They must be made into responsible men.

In modern societies the provider role is performed with money. But unlike the warrior's emblems and hunter's game, money lacks gender. Women can get it as well as men. The provider role, therefore, is losing its immediate sexual correlation. It is sustained by the greater desire of men to perform it and by their greater aptitude for competition. Together with the maternal concerns of most women, these male tendencies mean that married men, in general, earn much more money than married women. Money thus acquires a kind of ulterior sex in the context of marriage.

This ulterior gender of money breaks down among single people. The psychological need for single men to perform is not joined with a significantly greater ability to earn money. The bent of men to provide for women is not joined by a visible need of single women to be supported. At most of the jobs done by bachelors it is difficult for men to find the symbols of their ultimate jobs and purpose in life. The male groups that form in many job sites are poorly organized and powerless. The role of testing and selection is done by others, elsewhere, and is not experienced as a significant personal initiation, entailing discipline and responsibility to other men. Rather it often suggests impersonal responsibilities, without sexual meaning, to an abstract company or bureaucracy, time clock or administrator.

Single men, then, find little encouragement not to remain immature, uninitiated boys. They often stay that way, with the thirty- and forty-year-old bachelors exhibiting the same restless sense of incompletion as the teenager. For boys to grow up, modern society no longer relies chiefly on rites of provision, initiation, bonding, and sex roles. We try to replace them with schools and colleges and training courses. But they are not enough, because they fail to tap the inner sources of motivation and fail to respond to sexuality. Where education fails we turn to reformatories. They become schools for crime. We start psychiatric clinics. They work for a few. We turn in despair to mental hospitals. They work for fewer. We build prisons and fill them—then create programs for reform. Recent studies have shown, however, that no method of rehabilitation yet tried with large numbers of prisoners has been proved to affect recidivism in any measurable way.[13] As violence paralyzes many city schools, and as riots erupt in our prisons, and as mental hospitals decline into detention centers, we discover that there is only one institution left in our society that can succeed in dealing with young men: marriage and family.

In our society, love, sex, marriage, and family are the only hope of dealing with the crisis of single men, their violence and their disease. It is impossible to understand how the society can work unless one perceives the real role of family life, and unless one understands the reality and nature of love. To understand how single men grow up, one has to know how love works. The burden love bears in modern society is so great that it leaves the realm of poetry and enters the domain of religious faith.

11

How Love Works

The wild thyme unseen and wild strawberry,
The laughter in the garden, echoed ecstasy
Not lost, but requiring, pointing to the agony
Of death and birth.

— T. S. ELIOT

Eddie is a single man, tense and troubled. He has another beer and walks over to the jukebox. Two songs for a quarter. He grunts, returns to his seat. He is genuinely pissed off. There is no way the Knicks can catch 'em now, it'll be like 1969, you'll see. The Bullets will take it. This young guy, Chenier, don't tell anybody (this is New York) but he can play Walt Frazier dead even, no question. And he can *shoot*. Shit. Well, we'll see in the second half.

Until the last quarter, the Knicks remain behind. Then everything goes wrong for them—except Walt Frazier. But I mean, what else is there? The man's the greatest genius in the history of basketball. Fourteen out of the last sixteen points he scored, and he passed to Bradley for the other two. And then that steal in the end when he needed it. From Chenier! How can you beat that? No way. No way you're going to stop this man Saturday night in New York City.

He walks over to a couple of girls sitting in the corner. They have neat, glossy hairdos, one blonde, one brunette, look as if they just got off a plane after saying "so long,"

133

clicking the so-nice smile for a hundred passengers. "Coffee, tea, or me?" he asks, with an exaggerated bow. "Or do you want to use the sanitary receptacle . . . it is, let's see, it is *right* in front of you . . . in my pocket here." He fumbles in his pocket, oh, oh, a condom. He decides to leave it there, laughs at his private joke. The girls guffaw happily at his act. Yes, some days he can score from any point on the court, can't he; they all go in for Walt and me.

Some days, though, it's bad. Sluggish. Some days, Walt looks as though he doesn't really care. I mean I *know* the man's cool. But for three hundred thou, he should save his booze and broads for the off season. Shit, he even blows the foul shots.

Eddie yells to the bartender at the other end. "Turn that fuckin' thing off, will ya?"

"No, I'm watching," says the man to his right.

"So, fuck you," he responds, then reconsiders. "I'm just kidding, fella. Don't take it personal."

"You better be kidding."

"All right!" he waves to the bartender again. "Bill, could you please lower the sound. I want to play some music."

"I want the sound up," says the man next to him. Something turns in Eddie's stomach. The guy looks about five ten, frail. Eddie could take him, even sluggish. "So piss in your beer," he says.

"Just a damn minute," says the man. "Don't talk to me like that."

The bartender comes over. "What's going on here, any-way?"

"This guy here is drunk and abusive," says the man.

"It's all right, Bill. I'm okay." He looks at the man, tries to smile. "Forget it, will you. I'm sorry I said it."

"You better be."

"Well, both of you cool it," says the bartender.

There is a girl over by the jukebox, alone. The first

thing Eddie notices is the way her rear blooms under the skirt, lifting it so he could read the lines of the thighs above the nice calves. He doesn't need to notice any second thing. "Forget it, Bill," he says, "I got better things to think about than this creep." The man yaps behind him as Eddie gets up and walks over to the jukebox, but he doesn't follow.

"See any songs you'd like to play for me?" Eddie asks. She giggles. "How about 'Trouble Man,' Marvin Gaye," he suggests. "Yeah, all right, I like him," she says. He notices she is plain, but pleasant sexy plain. And a body. She would do very well. Very well. He begins to feel good. The hell with the Knicks.

"Where you sitting?" he asks.

"Oh, I'm with my boy friend over there in the corner," she says.

He goes back to the bar, at another place farther away. The bartender has turned down the sound on the T.V., so Eddie can't hear very well. Frazier is not himself tonight. You know, if I didn't know he was twenty-seven, I would say he was growing old, losing his reflexes.

"Gimme another beer, could you . . . please," he asks. Jesus, these beers add up. I guess it's the broads, though. They get to anyone after a while. Even to a cool black mother like Walt. Yeah, it's probably the broads. It sure as hell isn't the broads in here. You could live forever if all of them were as ugly as these, with boy friends in their corners. The score flashes on the screen. It's bad. The Knicks are down by twenty-two points. There's no chance tonight, he says to himself. He'd go home and get some sleep. He has to be in the supervisor's office at 9:00 A.M. the next morning. Boot-licking time. He wouldn't want to have beer on his tongue then . . .

"It's the vicarious virility problem," says Alex smoothly. "There are a million men, hell, thirty million men in America who try to live off the masculinity, the potency, of guys like Walt Frazier. But it won't work. A man has to have something himself. Right, Sally?" He smiles at the girl next to him on the couch. She's wearing jeans and a spangly tee-shirt. She beams back. Alex is thirty-one, living with Sally in a small, cluttered apartment near the Michigan State campus.

"Yeah, all I got left to do is finish my dissertation. Jesus, sometimes I think I'll never finish the thing." He turns to Sally. "Hey, you can go and do your homework now if you want—while I talk to this guy." He smiles benignly at her, then glances toward the next room.

"Well, it was good to meet you," she says to the visitor. She leaves, swinging her hips knowingly and closing the door behind her.

"I'm sorry to have to do that," Alex says, "but if we're going to talk frankly, well . . .

"Anyway, it's really hard getting any writing done while I hold a job at the same time. I'm counseling students at the high school. There's a real mess for you. They'd as soon knife you as read anything. Good kids, though, some of them. But I can't take that job much longer. Maybe I'll quit. Then my writing will go faster.

"Joan. Yes. Well, Joan and I never made it too well after the fight about the abortion. I mean, she's liberated, right? *She* messes up on her diaphragm. And then she's mad, because I'm not eager and thrilled to pay the bill. She's got as much money as I do. Anyway she moved out. Good riddance, I say.

"Lansing, Michigan. Do you realize there are people who actually live out their lives in this town? It's hard to believe. The winters are frigid and the springs last six weeks, and even in the spring all anybody ever talks about is the goddam football team. So it might as well be fall again—which means winter. Then they tell stories about previous football teams. Bubba Smith and his damn pink Cadillac, and his little brother, weighed two hundred and sixty-five pounds. Bubba must have been something else. But mostly it's just cold. They *got* to be the 'Spartans' just to survive it. This place is like a fox eating out my gut. You know I'm probably going to go back to L.A. to finish my writing. One good year in the sun and I'll be fine.

"One thing, though, I've learned in the last couple years. I sure in hell don't want to teach. Not in the high schools, the colleges, nowhere. I've met these guys, all obsessed with what the Department head thinks about them, or how stupid is some broad who got tenure, or how they can get into the textbook racket, or whether there is some opening maybe at North Dakota State. I've had it with teaching. When I get my doctorate I'm going to try to get a political job, maybe on a Senator's staff. I've always thought I might be able to go into politics myself someday. You know, they asked me to give a speech to the political club at the high school last month, and I really turned them on. I thought they would keep me talking all night. They kept asking questions. Those high school kids are all right, some of them. Look at Sally . . ."

Pete's friends in the group call him "Snooze" because he closes his eyes and lets his lower lip hang loose while he plays the drums. He is twenty-five years old. He is not yet a very good drummer. But then it is not a very good group. It specializes in "Gloria" and "Louie, Louie." They make a little money playing at high school dances and at an occasional party, and they have a gig on Tuesday and Wednesday nights at a local juice bar called The Blue Pumpkin. In a good month Snooze will make 150 dollars from his music.

He supplements it working at a local gas station, but he has just been laid off for the energy crisis, which he thinks is a plot between Richard Nixon and the Mobil Station across the street to suppress the revolution. He lives with a group, commune style, in an old reconditioned barn. Nonetheless, there is rent to pay and food, and pills. He wonders if he should try to sell grass again. "It grows like nothin' on the hill," he says.

But he is very concerned about the Mafia. Though there is no hope for him in the music business, he believes his future lies in song writing. Here is one of his songs on a political topic.

Where are you, Lee Oswald.
We need you today
To gun down Tricky Dicky,
To make the man pay.

Where are you, Sirhan Sirhan.
Come out of your cell.
Come on and get Ford now
And blast him to hell.

Come back, John Wilkes Booth.
You shot the wrong man.
Come back and kill Kissinger.
Don't let your gun jam.

Snooze wants to know if there have been any other assassins, so he can add new verses. "You have to have at least five verses for one of the big record companies to bite," he says authoritatively. He gives the impression of knowing his way around the world of music.

"Yeah, I know the music scene pretty good," he says. "All I need is a break—like James Taylor got. Just one break."

There are millions of single men like these three, unconnected to any promising reality, dissipating their lives by the years, moving from job to job, woman to woman, illusion to embitterment. Yet they are not hopeless. Many more millions have passed through the same slough, incurred the same boozy dreams, marijuana highs, acid crashes, sex diseases, job vapors, legal scrapes, wanderings. They follow the entire syndrome and then break out of it. Normally they do not escape through psychiatrists' offices, sex education courses, VISTA or

Peace Corps programs, reformatories, or guidance counseling uplift. What happens, most of the time—the only effective thing that happens, the only process that reaches the sources of motivation and character—is falling in love.

Love is effective because it works at a deeper, more in-stinctual level than the other modes of education and change. Love does not teach or persuade. It possesses and transforms. It is powerful because it is not superficial, because it arises from parts of the brain less variable and manipulable than ra-tionality. Love and marriage are products of 35 million years of evolution rather than a few years of instruction at school, a few hours of threats and promises from counselors and policemen, or a few months of unpleasant experiences with the singles life.

A man is depressed but not transfigured by a vision of forty years of dirty sheets and unmade mornings. It is not enough to see the light over a sleeping body without a remem-bered face. It is not enough to trudge home alone at three A.M.—after insults from three different women—thinking of the hangover at work just six hours hence. It should be enough, one would suppose, if men were reasonable and could be changed by reason alone.

But reason has a hundred voices: pointing plausibly to the flaws of each successive lover; depicting orgiastic futures for liberated singles; describing clinically the snares and pit-falls of marriage; disparaging choices that are made to be irrevocable in a life of changing sentiments and fortunes.

There are intelligent men and women making the case against wedlock and children. There are urbane professors expounding their eloquent dolor on the future of the race. There are reasonable projections of depression and holocaust, of petty dictators with doomsday machines. Why bring chil-dren into such a world? ask the coolly reasonable voices of Zero Population Growth.

If a society, or a man, turned to reason alone, the skies would be dense with the pale cast of thought and one would never see the sun. It is not just an intelligent appraisal of his circumstances that transforms the single man. It is not merely a desire for companionship or "growth." It is a deeper alchemy of change, flowing from a primal source. It seeps slowly into the flesh of his mind, from the memory of his bones, the glands of his spirit; it rises through a life, until it can ignite. It is a perilous process, full of chances for misfire and mistake—or for an ever more mildewed middle age. But most of human life is incomprehensibly complex and precarious, and our minds and bodies and societies have functioned for millennia without an inkling of understanding even among the men in charge. We still have little idea how or why works the human brain. But we have seen it work, and so have we seen love. Love infuses reason and experience with the power to change a man, caught in a morbid present, into a man passionately engaged with the future.

The man may not be receptive at first. The change that leads to love often comes slowly. Many of the girls he finds will not help. They tend to go along with him and affirm his single life. Most of the time, though, the singles circuit finally becomes insufferable, offering neither sexual fulfillment nor manhood.

One morning he turns to the body sleeping next to him, whose name he hardly knows, whose health he hardly trusts, and who has nothing to say to him, and he decides he has to find something better. One day he looks across the room over a pile of dirty dishes and cigarette butts and beer cans and sex magazines and bills and filthy laundry and he does not see the evidence of happy carousing and bachelor freedom; he sees a trap closing upon him more grimly than any marriage. One day while joking with friends about the latest of his acquaintances to be caught and hitched, he silently wonders, for a moment, whether he really wishes it were he.

Suddenly he has a new glimpse of himself. His body is beginning to decline, grow weaker and slower, even if he keeps it fit. His body, which once measured out his few advantages over women, is beginning to intimate its terrible plan to become as weak as an older woman's. His aggressiveness, which burst in fitful storms through his young life but never seemed to cleanse him—his aggression for which he could so rarely find the adequate battle, the harmonious chase —is souring now. His job, so below his measure as a man, so out of tune with his body and his inspiration, now stretches ahead without joy or relief. His sex, the force that drove the flower of his youth, drives still, drives again and again the same hard bargain—for which there are fewer and fewer takers, in a sexual arena with no final achievement for the single man, in which sex itself becomes work that is never done.

Such bleak visions are often necessary to break a man's grip on the illusions of his independence and sufficiency: the mark of the immaturity which one finds in so many single men and to which one sees so many divorced men try to regress. In the young ones, it may be "just a phase." But for some, it is a phase that does not end until too late. They find themselves trapped in a youth as corrosive as Dorian Gray's. They become the dirty old men. Or the pathetic middle-aged: hanging around discotheques, waiting for the slow dances— or gyrating like beached fish through the fast ones. Sometimes they have money and can buy whatever they want. What they cannot purchase is their own age.

The single man is caught on a reef and the tide is running out. He is being biologically stranded and he has a hopeless dream. Studs Terkel's book *Working* registers again and again men's desire to be *remembered*. Yet who in this world is much remembered for his job? Even the great are soon supplanted, and Walt Frazier knows he has to remain at the top of his game—*perform*, again and again—or Phil Chenier and a hundred others will rise to displace him. Memories fade. It is foolish to turn to one's work for immortality. We see men struggle gloriously on the reef—make a small dent in the darkness. It is often a good try and for a dozen men a generation it works for a while. But the only way off the reef, the only escape for the biologically stranded, the single man, is a woman. The water is wide, he cannot cross it alone; build him a boat that can carry two. His children will remember. They are the ones who are sure. They offer at least a hope.

The single man, stuck with what he may sense as a choice between being trapped and being stranded, still may respond by trying one more fling, perhaps with the new girl down the bar. The biological predicament can be warded off for a time, like Hemingway's hyena. But it cannot be denied. For its fumes transpire from below, from the regions of death. If he lives among them too long without letting them be burned away—for better or worse—he begins to die. We know the repertory. Death often appears in the guise of eternal youth, at the ever-infatuating fountains: alcohol, drugs, hallucinogenic sex. For a while we believe in the disguise. But the hyena returns and there is mortality in the air— diseases, accidents, concealed suicides, the whole range of the single man's aggression turned inward.

But where there is death, there is hope. For the man who is in touch with his mortality, but not in the grips of it, is also in touch with the sources of his love. He is in contact with the elements—the natural fires and storms that we so often use as metaphors for his passions. He is a man who can be deeply and effectively changed. He can find his age, his relation to the world, his maturity, his future. He can burn his signature into the covenant of a specific life.

The man has found a vital energy and a possibility of durable change. It has assumed the shape of a woman. It is the same form that has caught his eye and roiled his body all these years. But now there will be depths below the pleasing surfaces, meanings beyond the momentary ruttings. There will be a sense that this vessel contains the secrets of new life, that the womb and breasts bear a gestalt of immortality. There will be a knowledge that to treat this treasure as an object—a mere body the equal of his own, a mere matrix of his pleasure

—is to defile life itself. It is this recognition that she offers a higher possibility; it is this consciousness that he has to struggle to be worthy of her which finally issues the spark. And then arises the change that transcends his own death.

The man's love begins in a knowledge of inferiority, but it offers a promise of dignity and purpose. For he then has to create, by dint of his own effort, and without the miracle of a womb, a life that a woman could choose. Thus are released and formed the energies of civilized society. He provides, and he does it for a lifetime, for a life.

So the single man's aspiration assumes the shape of a woman. But in order to reach the fuller meanings, the procreative mysteries, he has to choose a specific woman for whom to perform. As I wrote in *Sexual Suicide:* "This recognition, the beginning of love, seems to be evoked by a man's desire, conscious or unconscious, to identify and keep his progeny. In a civilized society, he will not normally be able to claim his children if they are born to several mothers. He must choose a particular woman and submit to her if he is to have offspring of his own. His love defines his choice. His need to choose evokes his love. His sexual drive lends energy to his love and his love gives shape, meaning, and continuity to his sexuality. When he selects a specific woman, he in essence defines himself both to himself and in society. Every sex act thereafter celebrates that definition and social engagement."

The man is not conscious, much of the time, of the reasons for his commitment. As we know, the heart has its reasons. But any reasons of the heart are likely to spring from the primal human experiences, and the primal predicament of man—throughout the history of the race—has been the need to choose a particular woman and stay by her and provide for her, if he is to know his children and they are to love him and call him father.

When he chooses, he can change. He has to change, for

his wife will not long have him if he remains in spirit a single
man. He must settle his life, and commit it to the needs of
raising a family. In other words, he has to eschew his hunter's
sexuality—his life as a naked nomad—and adopt hers, defined by the possibility of bearing children.

For the woman's heart, too, has reasons, and they too
originate in a primal predicament. In fact, her reasons are
far more strongly imprinted than the man's, because until
recently she has never had a fully alternative life. There was
never a time in human evolution when she could long separate her sexuality from its consequences. Thus she evolved a
deeper and more elaborate sexual nature, leading from the
joys of orgasm on into the burdens and satisfactions of pregnancy, climaxing in the momentous and tumultuous throes
of labor and childbirth and extending into the quieter balms
of lactation and nurture, and, finally, leading to all the awesome responsibilities of mothering a vulnerable yet unique and
irreplaceable life.

These profound and overwhelming potentialities and experiences, undergone by every generation of human females
over all time, give the woman, as part of her very sexuality, a
sense of the future: a sense of evolution and growth, a notion
of deferring pleasures for future gains, a sense of the phases
and seasons of life, a devotion to the value of the individual
human being. These sentiments are the very source of human
morality. They comprise the biological roots of all human
social systems.

Anthropologists tell us that the pattern of monogamy is
less strongly rooted than the scheme of maternity, and that,
in fact, the man may still be biologically maladapted for it.
This may well be. But monogamy nonetheless lays claim to a
profound legacy of evolutionary experience for both sexes.
Corresponding to the man's awareness that he cannot fully be
a father without choosing a specific woman is the woman's
awareness that she cannot have a husband to protect her and
her children, and provide for them, unless she chooses a

specific man. So for all the competing appeals of promiscuity, male bonding, and domestic matriarchy, one may conclude that monogamy has a history sufficiently long and profound to sustain the system of marriage.

Through falling in love the single man rises to a new moral plane. Again, however, this does not happen as a result of a series of rational calculations. We still have no idea how to manufacture a moral being. The transformation can take root because he is in love, possessed. It is not enough merely to recognize his biological impasse, his culture of death; it is not enough merely to acknowledge a superior order of femininity and a desire for children. As every psychiatrist and most sentient humans have come to understand, knowledge alone will not often suffice to produce deep and enduring changes in human character. A man changes because of the crisis of his sexual compulsions and aggressive drives.

In falling in love, the single man has to shut off many former outlets for his energies. Promiscuous sex, male group aggressions, erratic cycles of intense activity and prolonged torpor have to give way to the more purposeful and more elaborate sexuality of the woman. What was once diffuse is suddenly and explosively concentrated. What was once allowed to follow its natural rhythm is now subjected to an ethic of responsibility. This is no minor event in his psyche. What is being concentrated and subdued are nothing less than the supreme drives of his manhood, to which his hormonal system is devoted and his brain adapted: his sex and his aggression.

Here we are not dealing in superficial conditions, of the sort manipulated in the programs of rehabilitation that have so sweepingly failed in prisons and other such institutions. Instead we are addressing directly the demonic energies that so often produce criminal or self-destructive behavior. Love changes, deepens and channels the flows of energy, emotion, and will that impel a man's most important commitments and most extreme behaviors. Thus his inner life can be trans-figured.

Nonetheless, the changes are sufficiently unstable so that the man cannot merely fall in love and be expected to live peacefully ever after. Corresponding to the changes in his inner life must come changes in his social environment. Love, and the morality of love, the woman's morality, must be institutionalized and the man must submit to the institution.

The cultural embodiment of these biological options is the institution of marriage. It is based on a recognition that the man's connection to the family and thus to civilized life is more precarious than the woman's. Thus marriage focuses on binding the man. It is the crucial institution of civilized life.

12

Why Men Marry

Around every bachelor of more than 35, legends tend to congregate, chiefly about the causes of his celibacy . . . . Such tales are nearly always moonshine. The reason why the average bachelor of thirty-five remains a bachelor is really very simple. It is, in brief, that no ordinarily attractive and intelligent woman has ever made a serious and undivided effort to marry him.

—H. L. MENCKEN

Ingrid Bengis, in her eloquent *cri de coeur, Combat in the Erogenous Zone,*[1] rises at the end of her chapter on "Man Hating" to ask the crucial questions: "Should I adjust to the 'facts of life' about the nature of the male species? Should men adjust to the facts of life about women? About me? And if neither of us can complete that adjustment, is the price we must pay an isolation so profound that real communion becomes all but impossible?"

Bengis fails to give answers to these questions, but they hover over every page. As she tells of her anguish, one wishes she would reach out and grasp them.

Bengis describes her sexuality as subtle and intense, thriving on a range of sensuous experiences beyond intercourse and dependent on familiarity and love. Male sexuality, she usually discovers, is a simple and compulsive drive to orgasm, combined with a yen for the road. While sex normally

147

heightens her desire for the man, she is distressed to find it often drains the man of passion for her.

Are these conflicts a terrible joke of nature, she wonders, or has she never met the right men? She thinks she has tried everything. At the time of her writing she had had several love affairs, and gone on bouts of promiscuity, "combat," lesbianism ("she made my blood feel like marmalade") and even a transatlantic, ultramontane, tri-monthly commuting relationship. Now she is trying abstinence. But it won't last either, so she implies, in her final and poignant apostrophes to love and permanence.

I am glad that she did not resolve her perplexities, transcend her aporias of liberation. For from them issues, as an allegedly feminist testament, a most powerful and convincing affirmation of monogamous love. She does not explicitly celebrate monogamy. But it is the only place for her to turn, and the heroine of the erogenous zone, after all her tossing to and fro, seems ready at last to "discover that the world is round"—which she quotes Doris Lessing as suggesting is the destination of most learning. You end up where you began, but at a higher point on the spiral. The woman in the book seems ready to enter the central arena of the struggle between the sexes—and win.

Because the answer is that the woman has to win. The man has to adjust to the woman. If you have something as complex and exalted as Ingrid Bengis's sexuality—indeed, female sexuality itself—you do not make it adjust to the crude and simple impulses of a man. You do not move Ingrid into Relaxation Plus or make her pose for the *Playboy* centerfold. You try to find some way of refining, sublimating, deepening, and extending male sexuality, adapting it to hers. Otherwise you have an image of sex as the anguished combat, which Bengis envisages in her book. Or you have the Victorian image of sex as a wastage and despoliation of women, to which the only answers are grin-and-bear-it or chastity.

There are better possibilities. Most of us know that sex does not have to bring a deficit to the human account, a loss of human potentiality. We know that the process by which we biologically perpetuate the race does not have to spiritually deplete it. We see the more modest labors of centuries of men devoted to serving its ultimate institution, the family.

In fact, it can be argued that the very achievement of human civilization rests on that submission of male to female nature. The men have to leave their battles and hunts and whorings and commit their energies to the building and supporting of homes and the celebration of women. They do it erratically and imperfectly, but they do it nonetheless, and sometimes enough so that civilizations emerge.

This miraculous transformation of men has been accomplished by millions of women far less endowed in mind and body than our heroine. Why does she fail? She fails because the men she knows are single and she is a "liberated woman." That is to say, she is a woman who does not convey to the men with whom she consorts a desire to marry and have children. Much of the time she merely adjusts to their sexuality of limited copulation and then hates the men for abusing hers. But it is not they, but she, who is degrading her sexuality. She is degrading it in the guise of "liberation" from its higher, and more exacting, and arduous possibilities. She really understands this, and says as much in her book.

A man in an affair is usually looking to go on. Unless he believes that the relationship is going to change his life, he is often not interested in prolonging it. He is still in the spirit of the chase, and it is more interesting for him to try another woman than to continue with one, however beautiful, who is unavailable to him in some profound way. A single man is still a hunter, and his relationships with women follow a rhythm of pursuit and conquest. Once he has conquered her in his way, the woman has to show a desire to conquer him on her terms. Otherwise the relationship will seem static to the

man and thus in danger of deteriorating. He fears the woman
may leave; or more specifically he may fear a loss of his own
sexual powers, leading to the woman's departure. He is simply
not going to be interested in an extended exchange of sweet
sentiments in the spirit of the lesbian relationships that Bengis
describes.

This is because the man, though more intense and sexually aggressive than the woman, is also more limited. The
woman has to suggest the directions of the evolution of love—
all the phases between initial sexual exchange and the desire
to consummate and embody it with children and future. If
the woman is resolute and the man loves her, he is usually
capable of learning; he ultimately will want to.

What has to happen is that the love of the man, which in
itself is a tribute to feminine superiority, is eventually institutionalized. He must not be allowed to entertain the idea that
he is still a single man, whose highest enjoyment comes in the
capture of another woman. He must become a married man.
It will make a great difference. Nothing else will do as much
to get the man to concentrate on responding as variously and
fully as he can to the needs of the woman. That is the purpose
of the institution—to break the hold of the hunt and the male
group and make the man attend to more important matters: a
woman and her children.

Marriage works because the man is asked to change his
essential sexuality only as part of a clear scheme for replacing
it with new masculine roles. In affairs, as they are extended,
the man often feels absorbed by the woman's sexuality without
being granted any balancing masculinity. He is not essentially
a provider or protector, let alone a father. He feels his essential remaining male role is as stud. Yet without other masculine support, he performs the stud role best when he is in pursuit, constantly being excited by new women, new challenges.
The woman must show him the larger possibilities of the relationship at hand, and show how he is needed in her life as a

man. It can be done without marriage. But marriage is by far the most enduringly dependable way.

In broad social terms, in fact, it is the only way. Ms. Bengis often writes as if the only purpose of society is to discover and accommodate the most "authentic" impulses of its members. Yet one of the strongest aspects of her book is the evidence it offers that the individual, alone and "free," disintegrates. Authenticity is achieved socially, and the society must induce the vast majority of its members to follow predictable and responsible lives, taking care of each other and their children, and disciplining male aggression. Whether or not all women, in their most ineffable marmalade, are in some sense lesbian is irrelevant. If they are, the society does well to socialize it out of them—except for a small minority—just as it tries to limit male homosexuality, which is a much more serious, less reversible disorder. Marriage is the crucial institution. It mobilizes biology, economics, psychology, love, aggression, aspiration, optimism, to transfigure the man and his sexuality.

When the man submits his limited sexual impulse to the woman's, he is adopting a higher, more extended, mode of sexual life. He is submitting, that is, to the values of maternal morality and futurity.

The single man has a deep inner sense of dispensability, perhaps evolved during the millennia of his service in the front lines of tribal defense. He is sexually optional. Several dominant males could impregnate all the women and perpetuate the tribe. It is this sense of dispensability that makes the single man a good fighter, a good crusader, a good martyr. But it also weakens his ability to care deeply and long and stunts his sense of the preciousness of human beings. Because the woman has always been directly responsible for infants, and almost always exclusively responsible, she is dubious about the dying and killing that have surrounded the male groups. When the man submits to female sexuality, therefore, he not only adopts an ethic of long-term responsibility for the life and death matters of his own children's upbringing but he also adopts a new perspective on life and death itself. His life is no longer so optional, because his wife and children depend on him. Thus individual life assumes a higher value within the monogamous marriage than it does in the male group.

When a man gets married, the changes in his life go far beyond his immediate relationship. Statistically, his college grades summarily climb above those of more talented singles, his crime rate plummets, he pays his bills, and qualifies for credit. He drives more carefully and qualifies for cheaper insurance. His income as much as doubles. He becomes much more psychologically stable. Contrary to the theory that breadwinning duties account for high male mortality, he lives much longer than his counterpart who stays single. And, of course, in most cases he devotes himself sexually to one woman.

The evidence comes in many forms. Mohammad Ali reaches for a kind of puritanical statesmanship. Stokely Carmichael settles in a stately mansion in Georgetown. Ringo Starr buys a tie and cuts his hair. Mario Savio becomes a professor of political theory. Dave Wottle takes off his hat. One could continue the list indefinitely, with changes more far-reaching. Marriage, in fact, is the most consistently effective variable in all the tables of the Census, of the National Center for Health Statistics, and of every insurance company and credit agency. It also can be the most telling change that a man undergoes.

No such significant changes occur in a woman's temperament, longevity, or behavior. The unmarried woman is already more stable and responsible than the single man. What has happened is that the single man has subordinated his sexuality to hers. Because his sexuality is so intimately bound up with all his other rhythms and motives, this change transforms his entire psychology, so that it actually becomes in essence much like the woman's.

The agony of divorced men further reveals the centrality of the marriage tie. It is not a mere withdrawal of their domestic amenities that brings about the immense increase in diseases, mental and physical, and in deaths from every cause, from suicides to coronaries. Nor is it a mere withdrawal of sex, for as the *Playboy* figures suggest—and the Census statistics document—there may be ample opportunities for sex with the vast numbers of middle-aged divorced women. In fact, divorced men often go on a sexual binge after their marriage breakup. The problem of divorced men is not domestic or narrowly "sexual." It is their sense of being uprooted from their very lives. The connections by which their psychology was shaped as young men are broken. They find themselves as older hunters, unwanted on the chase, even their relations with their children now ambiguous and conflicting.

The lucky ones manage to recover and reestablish themselves. Often, however, the new relationships, even new marriages, lack a feeling of continuity and future. Their new wives are like balms to their psychic wounds and the men discover that their needs are deeper than the salves can reach. They want a sense that, as they grow old, they are not growing out of their lives; that they are not breaking all the bonds that shaped their will and vitality, pulled them out of bed in the morning and brought them home at night, which gave meaning and resonance to their unheroic daily lives. These ties, because they were tempered in the sexual crucible of young manhood, became a central part of the man's sexual identity. He can no more escape them than he can escape the memories of his infancy and childhood. His family becomes an essential part of what he is, and thus for better or worse his wife is, and will always be, a part of him. His new adult sexuality has been formed through hers. He cannot leave her without tearing his own life's fabric.

The institution of marriage is not a mere domestic convenience. In modern society it has become a necessity for most men. Thus the ones who are not married—or whose marriages collapse—become "single men" in all their dubious glory. They find themselves exiles from the natural chain of life, their sexuality nearly meaningless without love. A mother can bear and love a child with only the most passing contact with a man. Without love, the man is able only to screw. He can do it a lot, but after his first years it will only get him un-threaded, and in the end he is disconnected and alone.

As a social institution, marriage transcends individual predicaments. The health of a society, its collective vitality, ultimately resides in its concern for the future, its sense of a connection with generations to come. There is perhaps no morè important index of the social condition. It is the very temperature of a community. A community preoccupied with the present, obsessed with an immediate threat or pleasure, is enfevered. A social body, as a human body, can run a very high fever for short periods in order to repel a specific threat or to meet an emergency, a war or domestic crisis. But if it finds itself perpetually enfevered, it begins to run down and can no longer provide for its future. Its social programs can fail to work, its businesses fail to produce, its laws become unenforceable. The will and morale and community of its people can founder. A society, apparently working well, can stand impotent before its most important domestic and exter-nal threats and opportunities.

The sense of social vitality and balance does not "just happen." In civilized conditions it is normally love, marriage, and the nurture of children that project a society into the future and make it responsible for posterity. There does not seem to be any other dependable way to do it, throughout an entire population over time. Militarism, chauvinism, religious fanaticism, even the leadership of a charismatic psychopath can serve briefly, and at a major cost to individual freedom. But in general it is only through love for specific children that a society evokes long-term commitments from its members.

That is why the social temperature of single men is so

high—why they end up so often being sent to war or jail or other institutions, and why they burn out so young. A society does not run into real trouble, however, until its culture begins to adopt the single male pattern; until the long-term commitments on which any enduring community is based are undermined by an opportunistic public philosophy. The public philosophy of the single man focuses on immediate gratification. "What did posterity ever do for me?" A society that widely adopts this attitude is in trouble, and American society is beginning to run a fever.

One reflection is the casual way in which people disclaim concern for the future. "I have no interest in having children." "Tomorrow never comes." The fetish is "now"—now fashions, now people. The lack of a sense of phase and growth and season suggests a preoccupation with the immediate, which knows no season. The fear of aging and the disdain for the wisdom of elders demonstates a similar attempt to defy at once both the learning of the past and the aging process in each individual. Drugs, acid, loveless sex all show a fevered impatience, an unwillingness to *wait,* to work, for the future.

This attitude is infecting the culture. Movies, plays, books, musical works all reveal a shallowness of reach and feeling, a high surface excitement but few deeper complexities. Above all, there is little comprehension of love, which in its optimism and faith is the sentiment of futurity. While the reality of the single life remains destructive, the fantasies of the single man pervade our popular culture.

Here there is no lack of male groups and aggressions, no lack of sexual immediacy, no lack of the warrior and the hunting mystiques. What is missing in most of our films and much of our recent literature is a sense of the denseness and complexity of human relationships, the long evolution of character, the sweep of time and change, the intricate shifts and connections of life and plot. Love and family and history are all lost in the voracity of the moment.

And what is lost is the very essence of the human drama in a working society. We resort to technology to compensate, and our films are more impressively produced than ever. Our novels and poems resort to technical virtuosity and surface complexity. Our art and music experiment with new media and materials. And all tend to resort to shocks and sensations, sex and violence, to conceal the fact that nothing is really happening. Nothing is growing or developing or changing. As art, it is, in a literal sense, unregenerate.

This is the ultimate barrenness of the single life. Nothing really happens. The past is meaningless and the future irrelevant. The present is boring, because it does not flow from a significant past or into a connected future. It has no plot or development of character. Because it is not dependent on anyone, or responsible for anyone, it does not care. So drama is lost as well.

It is taken for granted by many Americans that freedom and independence are what people need most. Our history proclaims it, our songs celebrate it, our culture extols it. How can young people growing up in America escape its siren appeal? It is the central problem of *Combat in the Erogenous Zone:* People imagine they can be free in love and sex. But it is impossible. Sexuality and love are inexorably feelings of dependency and responsibility. One feels oneself a man or a woman in the presence of the always unattainable complement. One is dependent on the other because one can never become it, and one senses its incompleteness. One loves the other because it is different and finally mysterious. If it becomes part of your life—if love and complex sexuality are achieved—you rely on their presence. You are enriched but you are bonded, and when you divide, however carefully, the increment of your life together, of your love and sexuality, bleeds out.

You can be free and independent, if you wish. Single men are free and independent. But you cannot also be loving and sexual. This is true of both sexes. But it is supremely true of men in modern society.

As the illusion of male independence declines, the problem will become the maintenance of a distinctive masculinity, the perpetuation of the masculine principle in our life as a society. Without it, the feminine principle will decline as well and we will be back where we started, as separate and diminished entities.

It is fortunate, therefore, that the great sexual dependence of men on women will continue to be counteracted, to some extent, by aspects of female dependence on a continued masculinity in men. Most of the crucial male roles can work, in varying forms, in future societies. They work, however, chiefly for men who are married.

Men will remain physically stronger and more dispensable. Thus they will tend to be more physically courageous. The role of protector will not retain the urgency and primacy it held on the frontier; it will not always be exercised through the threat of violence. But in all the continuing confrontations of daily life, only the smallest proportion of which can be mediated by the police or other authorities, the role of the male protector will continue to have value. Male insistence, self-assertion, toughness will be useful for any couple in a difficult, competitive world.

The role of the provider may be shared with the woman in many instances, but the trends are not nearly as clear as is widely believed. Women still enter the career arena in a more provisional and uncompetitive way than men. On the average, they still have less than half as much experience in their jobs and earn only about 60 percent as much money as men. This is not chiefly an effect of discrimination. It is an effect of greater male aggressiveness, biologically endowed; of greater male reliance on work for sexual identity, whether through male bonding, competition, or a role as provider; and greater male responsibility for "dependents"—wives who are diverted from the workplace and children who have increasing needs for education and support. The role of provider, for all the sensational theorizing to the contrary, will continue into the foreseeable future to be a masculine theme. Women may excel men in many areas, but most of them are unlikely to devote their lives chiefly to the competitive earning of money and status.

It does not appear that anything novel can be done, either, about the male role as sexual initiator and performer. It stems from biological realities and can only be overthrown with severe risk of what is known in the sex clinics as "dysfunction." The male sexual role, however, should be distinguished from the role of stud. With love, the man attains a position as father, which is respected by his wife and children. The role of father is of vital importance. It is not a matter of assimilating the mother's role, as is often supposed.

The love of the father has a different texture and feel than the love of the mother. There is a greater authority and discipline in it. It need not be remote or authoritarian, but it need not focus on infant nurturance either.

The father role should continue, in other words, in much the way it has, with one important distinction. With increasing leisure time, a man can be home much more often and be more available to the children. Since both boys and girls with strong paternal relationships also tend to have the happiest sexual lives and marriages, the presence of a father in the home can offer a good antidote to the problems of single men and marriages. Studies have consistently shown that men and women without fathers tend to have low "marital aptitudes" and reproduce the broken fabric of their own childhoods.

There is an irony in the life of the single man today. Although the culture depicts masculinity as a domain of the single—and although many married men still imagine a truly virile bachelorhood—the fact is that in modern society virile masculinity, too, is reserved chiefly for the married. The single man must find it as he can, and for many the arena of testing will be the competition for women. It is a harsh ground, tougher in many ways than the public rituals of old, but better rewarded too, by fuller and more intimate marriages. This is the goal for which the single man has to develop his masculinity, not for some equestrian dream of independence, but for the attainment of a higher sexuality, which can come in family life.

The purple light still flickers in the darkness, as did Gatsby's green one. But there is no orgiastic future, and its pursuit is as perilous and destructive as ever. Above all, there is no "love unlimited," except God's. Here on earth all love is a product of bounds, of dependencies, of balances, of limits. Nothing can testify as well to that reality as the current condition of free and independent single and divorced men in America.

Epilogue

The Nudist on the Beach

The great cloud wagons move
Outward still, dreaming of a Pacific.
LOUIS SIMPSON

When I was about three quarters of the way through this book—inveighing against sexual revolution, as I recall—a nude moved onto the beach below the house. I was told that she was a nudist. With my binoculars, I ascertained the absence of clothing, but no evidence of ideology. Later I saw her march down the sand, shoulders back, head held ideologically high, her hair flowing behind her like a banner in the wind. Yes, a nudist.

She had chosen this particular place, I suppose, because it is private. Nudism is illegal on the island, but one can get to this part only by boat or by a difficult trek along a rocky coast. The subtropical French are not known for vigorous post-prandial walks and the police are fully occupied in guarding the jail and avoiding *le voleur*. The nudist would be seen only by terns and pelicans, the Salazars and me. She would be disturbed by no one, except possibly me. And I had just two weeks in which to finish my work. I could not dally with a nudist.

Still, I rather looked forward to her departure. Her presence just below the balcony where I did my writing was a distraction. I wanted to *write* about naked nomads, not have

160

one on my doorstep. But at the end of the day she produced a little blue tent and lay down in it. Night fell, the winds howled, and I wrote on my illuminated balcony while she slept alone below me in the darkness on the sand. She seemed strangely vulnerable and romantic to me. I wondered if she thought of me as I was thinking of her, in my circle of light above the beach.

The next day I took a run, the first since my fall, and ended it at her tent. She was not there, but her belongings caught my eye. Among them was a French–English dictionary and a copy of the collected stories of Joseph Conrad. In the back, next to a small flashlight, was a large hunting knife. I glanced around the beach but did not see her. I swam for a while and then climbed back up to the house.

I learned that the nudist had crossed the Atlantic alone in a small sailboat. Her boat had been damaged in the voyage and could not be repaired. This day she had gone to town to arrange for a return trip to France. Later in the afternoon she reappeared on the beach. She studied her book with her head in the tent and her rear glowing red in the reddening sunlight.

Again that night she was there in the roaring darkness, invisible below my balcony, as I struggled on with chapters on testosterone and predatory hunters. I wondered what kind of Frenchwoman would sail across the Atlantic alone, reading the stories of Conrad in English.

The next day I ran again, and again ended up on the beach near her tent. This time she was there. Proximity did her no special favors. She was a large blonde with a broad, open face and a faint nervous twitch in her smile. She was not the kind of girl you would choose to have in a small boat with you as you crossed the Atlantic, unless you thought you needed her to help fight off the sharks. But she had a lot to say about naked nomads. At first I misinterpreted some of it, because I took her to be referring continually to "silly bastards," and I was tending to go along. Then she explained

that the word is *célibataires*—"single people" in French—and
said that she was one of them.

"I would never get married," she said in a hurried
French that suggested a life of getting things across to people
who were leaving her. "Never, never. It is stupid today. You
never know tomorrow, and there are so many places to go.
Today I am here, tomorrow I may be here again. Or I might
be on my way to South America, or France. Who knows what
will happen, even on this beach? I just wait and travel. Everything changes. Past and future are nothing. I just lie on the
beach in the sun. Maybe I will get a ride somewhere nice.
Who knows? Another year I do something else. Marriage
never. Once I lived with a man. Everything was cramped. I
left. I am twenty-five. You can sit down if you like."

I decided I had better get away myself, so I left her on
the beach and went back up to the house to have dinner and
write another chapter. As I labored away that night, I thought
of her, a stranded woman, nude and alone in the darkness,
living between sand and sea, with a knife by her hand as she
slept, waiting for someone to come, a boat, a man, another
year, the tide.

Notes

Prologue—On the Rocks

1. Statistics computed from U.S. Bureau of the Census, *Current Population Reports,* Series P-20, No. 255, "Marital Status and Living Arrangements: March 1973," U.S. Government Printing Office, Washington D.C., 1973: pp. 11–15 (Table 1. Marital Status by Age, Race, Farm-Nonfarm Residence, and Sex: March 1973 and 1970). Figure for intact families computed from ibid., p. 1–2. Marriage and divorce rate statistics from 1920 to 1965 appear in Hugh Carter and Paul C. Glick, *Marriage and Divorce: A Social and Economic Study,* American Public Health Association Vital and Health Statistics Monographs, Cambridge, Massachusetts: Harvard University Press, 1970: p. 41 and Chapter 3, passim. This book begins, "Probably few people realize that for every unit of increase since 1940 in the proportion divorced among adults . . . there have been five units of increase in the proportion married." Marriage, divorce, and remarriage figures since 1965 appear in Monthly Vital Statistics Reports of the National Center for Health Statistics, Rockville, Maryland. For summary and sources see: Paul C. Glick and Arthur J. Norton, "Perspectives on the Recent Upturn in Divorce and Remarriage." *Demography,* Volume 10, Number 3, August 1973: 301–314.
2. Glick and Norton, ibid., p. 302, 303 (Table 1).
3. Computed from statistics in "Marital Status and Living Arrangements: March 1973," op. cit. pp. 11–15.
4. "Is the American Family in Danger?" *U.S. News and World Report,* April 16, 1973: 71. However this 40 percent figure seems high when compared to statistics in Glick and Norton, op. cit. p. 302, which indicate an increase in the remarriage rate of slightly under 30 percent between the 1960–62 and the 1969–71 periods.
5. Glick and Norton, "Frequency, Duration, and Probability of Marriage and Divorce", *Journal of Marriage and The Family,*

May 1971: 310. Marriages among blacks and teenagers are much more likely to end in divorce. Glick and Norton write in their August 1973 report, "Perspectives on the Recent Upturn in Divorce and Remarriage," op. cit., p. 311: "(Our) single most important conclusion . . . is that between one in four and one in three women around 30 years old today are likely to experience divorce during their lifetime." They warn that all such predictions are highly uncertain. However, if the three most divorce prone categories (blacks, career professional women, and women married as teenagers) are removed from the statistics, the likelihood of divorce appears to be around 15 percent for a couple marrying today.

6. "Roundup of Current Research", *Society,* Vol. 11, No. 3, March/April 1974: 6.

1—Single Man Blues

1. Marion Clark, "So Much Trouble", *Potomac,* Sunday, April 14, 1974: 17 and passim.
2. Statistics computed from U.S. Bureau of the Census, Census of Population: 1970. MARITAL STATUS, Final Report PC (2)-4C, p. 1 (Table 1. Age of Persons 14 Years Old and Over, by Marital Status, Whether Married More Than Once, Whether Known to Have Been Widowed or Divorced, Race, and Sex: 1970). U.S. Government Printing Office, Washington, D.C. 1972.
3. Statistics computed from ibid. and from U.S. Bureau of the Census, Census of Population: 1970. SUBJECT REPORTS, Final Report PC (2)-4E, *Persons in Institutions and Other Group Quarters,* Government Printing Office, Washington, D.C. 1973: p. 27 (Table 16, Marital Status and Marital History of Inmates of Institutions 14 Years Old and Over by Age, Sex, and Race: 1970).
4. Statistic computed from U.S. Bureau of The Census, Census of Population: 1970. SUBJECT REPORTS, Final Report PC (2)-6A, *Employment Status and Work Experience.* U.S. Government Printing Office, Washington, D.C. 1973: p. 67 (Table 5, Marital Status by Labor Status, Age, Race and Sex).
5. Ibid. p. 302 (Table 20, Weeks Worked in 1969 and 1959 of Males 14 Years Old and Over by Marital Status, Age, and Race: 1970 and 1960).
6. MARITAL STATUS, op. cit., p. 181 (Table 7, Income in 1969 of Persons 14 Years Old and Over by Marital Status, Whether

Married More Than Once, Whether Known to Have Been Widowed or Divorced, Age, Race and Sex: 1970).

7. U.S. Bureau of The Census, *Current Population Reports,* Series P-20, No. 255, "Marital Status and Living Arrangements: March 1973," U.S. Government Printing Office, Washington, D.C., 1973, pp. 11–12 (Table 1. Marital Status by Age, Race, Farm-Nonfarm Residence, and Sex: March 1973 and 1970).

8. Statistic computed from data in U.S. Bureau of The Census, *Current Population Reports,* Special Studies, "Differences Between Income of White and Negro Families by Work Experience of Wife and Region: 1970, 1969, and 1959." Series P-23, No. 39, December 1971. Compare with: MARITAL STATUS, op. cit., p. 187, and Daniel P. Moynihan, "The Schism in Black America," *Public Interest,* Spring 1972: 10–11, and Ben J. Wattenberg and Richard M. Scammon, "Black Progress and Liberal Rhetoric," *Commentary,* April 1973: 35–44. When one excludes Southern blacks and single men from black statistics and includes welfare incomes, black incomes are close to white incomes. It is U.S. government policy, however, not the alleged "black tradition of matriarchy," that explains the high proportion of black men who are single. For fuller discussion of these issues, see Gilder, *Sexual Suicide.* New York: Quadrangle/New York Times Book Co., 1973, pp. 110–127. The best way to get men, white or black, to make the sacrifices necessary to earn large incomes, is to make them indispensable providers. Two reasons why black men do not feel themselves to be indispensable providers are (1) Aid For Families With Dependent Children (AFDC) payments which exceed the minimum wage for large families and (2) black female income is much closer to black male income than white female income is to white male income. See: Hearings before the Joint Economic Committee, Ninety Third Congress, First Session, Part 1, July 10, 11, 12, *Economic Problems of Women,* U.S. Government Printing Office, Washington, 1973, p. 96.

9. Ibid, pp. 20, 34–35, 47–48. Statements by Marina Whitman, of The Council of Economic Advisers, and by staff assistant June O'Neill, interpreting the National Longitudinal Survey sponsored by The U.S. Department of Labor, as analyzed by Jacob Mincer and Solomon Polachek. The survey compared the hourly earnings in 1966 of men and women between 30 and 44 in terms of experience and other qualifications. The survey showed that even in 1966 single women earned 86 percent as much as comparable *married* men and approximately the same as or more than

comparable single men. Marina Whitman, ignoring the figures for single men, contended that discrimination accounts for between 10 and 20 points of the overall percentage gap between male and female incomes. Her assumption is that without discrimination, women would earn exactly the same as married men rather than 86 percent as much. Thus she fails to consider the greater need and motivation of married men or the impact of testosterone. Nor does she mention the socialization of women against competing with men. If one considers these factors at all, the amount of demonstrable wage discrimination against women appears negligible, and the possibility arises that in many fields there is "discrimination" against men. The real explanation, however, is not "discrimination" but the kind of sex role differentiation that exists everywhere in the world.

10. MARITAL STATUS, op. cit., pp. 181–252 (Tables 7, 8, and 9) and U.S. Bureau of the Census, Census of Population: 1970. SUBJECT REPORTS, Final Report PC (2)-6A *Employment Status and Work Experience,* pp. 302–311 (Tables 20 and 21, Weeks Worked in 1969 and 1959 of Males [of Females] 14 Years Old and Over by Marital Status, Age, Race [and Presence of own Children] 1970 and 1960).

11. Computed from U.S. Department of Labor, unpublished data, "Median Income in 1972 of Persons by Years of School Completed by Sex"; and MARITAL STATUS op. cit., pp. 227–252 (Table 9) and pp. 181–222 (Table 7). Since, of all the agencies analyzing "discrimination" against women, not one chooses to compare their earnings directly with those of fully comparable single men, it is impossible to determine the exact income differences between the two groups in terms of experience and qualifications. But some evidence suggests that single men earn less than single women of the same age, qualifications, and work experience. In general, full time female workers have a median of less than half as many years in their current jobs as male workers. See *Economic Problems of Women,* op. cit., Part 2: 296.

12. MARITAL STATUS, op. cit., pp. 227–252 (Table 9).

13. Ibid.

14. Lester Thurow, "Education and Economic Equality," *Public Interest,* Summer 1972.

15. Christopher Jencks et al., *Inequality,* New York: Basic Books, 1972.

16. Phyllis Chesler, *Women and Madness.* Garden City. N.Y.; Doubleday, 1972.

17. Ibid., pp. 312–313 (Table 4) and passim.
18. Computed from data in *Persons in Institutions and Other Group Quarters,* op. cit.: pp. 7–8 (Table 4, Age of Patients in Mental Hospitals and Residential Treatment Centers by Type of Control, Sex, Race and Spanish Origin: 1970).
19. Ibid., pp. 2–5.
20. Chesler, op. cit., p. 324.
21. Jessie Bernard, *The Future of Marriage,* New York: World Publishing Company, 1972: pp. 295–316.
22. Ibid., Table 1 (Health of Men by Marital Status and Age, Health Defined in Terms of Absence of Chronic Condition or Restricted Activity). Unpublished Table, National Center for Health Statistics. Data are from 1968 Health Interview Survey.
23. Ibid., p. 318. Data from H. J. Gross, "The Depression-Prone and Depression-Resistant Sibling: A Study of 650 Three-Sibling Families: A Follow-up Note on Marital Status," *British Journal of Psychiatry* 114 (December 1968): 1559. See also Alistair Munro, "Some Familial and Social Factors in Depressive Illness," *British Journal of Psychiatry* 112 (May 1966): 440.
24. Kitogawa and Hauser, *Differential Mortality in the U.S.,* American Public Health Association, Vital and Health Statistics Monographs, 1960 Census Monograph Series, chapter on "Differential Mortality in The United States": pp. 108–113. See also: Hugh Carter and Paul C. Glick, *Marriage and Divorce: A Social and Economic Study.* American Public Health Association, Vital and Health Statistics Monographs, Cambridge, Massachusetts: Harvard University Press, 1970: 324–357 (Marital Status and Health); and Canadian Mortality According to Marital Status, By Sex [and age group] (Death Rate per 100,000 during 1969–1970), *Statistical Bulletin*, Metropolitan Life Insurance Company, August 1973. The Canadian figures are the most up to date examination of mortality by marital status. The latest U.S. figures, cited by Carter and Glick, come from The National Center for Health Statistics, *Mortality From Selected Causes by Marital Status, United States,* PHS Pub No 1000, Ser 20 No. 8. Washington D.C., Government Printing Office, 1970. This study is based on data collected in 1959–1961 and corrected by Carter and Glick for distortions in totals for the widowed and divorced. The marriage rate figures come from Carter and Glick, op. cit., pp. 40–77 and from other sources listed in Note 1 of the Prologue of this book.
25. Bernard, op. cit., Tables 5 and 12. From National Center for Health Statistics, Selected Symptoms of Psychological Distress

(U.S. Department of Health, Education and Welfare, 1970), Table 17, pp. 30–31.

26. Bernard, op. cit., Tables 8 and 30.
27. Ibid., Tables 3, 13, and 15.
28. Ibid., Table 3.
29. Martin S. Weinberg and Colin J. Williams, *Male Homosexuals, Their Problems and Adaptations,* New York: Oxford University Press, 1974: pp. 105–118.
30. Ibid., pp. 111–113.
31. "Playboy Panel: Homosexuality," *The Sensuous Society.* Chicago: Playboy Press, 1973, p. 85.
32. Weinberg and Williams, op. cit., p. 118.
33. Ibid., p. 116.
34. Ibid., pp. 105–118, 223–233, and passim. See also: Edward R. Sagarin, "On Homosexuality," *Contemporary Sociology, a journal of reviews,* American Sociological Association, Volume 2, Number 1, January 1973: pp. 3–13; and Arno Karlen, *Sexuality and Homosexuality, A New View,* New York: W. W. Norton & Co.: 1971. Sagarin offers an intelligent and comprehensive overview of recent literature on homosexuality. Karlen's book is by far the most ambitious, comprehensive and readable of recent books on the subject, but it is flawed by a simplistic view of sexuality as an arbitrary social construct and by a deceptive and clichéd presentation of anthropological evidence.
35. Computed from data in *Persons in Institutions and Other Group Quarters,* op. cit.: 49–53 (Table 26).
36. Carter and Glick, op. cit.: 338.
37. *Persons in Institutions* . . . op. cit.: 42–48 (Table 25).
38. Ibid.
39. Ibid., pp. 36–41 (Table 24).
40. Ibid.

2—Death of a Single Man

1. Hugh Carter and Paul C. Glick, *Marriage and Divorce: A Social and Economic Study.* American Public Health Association Vital and Health Statistics Monographs, Cambridge, Massachusetts: Harvard University Press, 1970: pp. 347 and 352. These statistics may significantly inflate results for widowed and divorced and thus underrate mortality of single men. For explanation and corrections, see Kitogawa and Hauser, *Differential Mortality in the U.S.,* American Public Health Association, Vital and Health Statistics Monographs, 1960 Census Monograph Series: pp.

108–113. For more recent data, see Canadian Mortality According to Marital Status, by Sex [and age group] (Death Rate per 100,000 during 1969–70), *Statistical Bulletin,* Metropolitan Life Insurance Company, August 1973. For supporting data from 19th-Century Europe, including France, Switzerland, Italy, Prussia, Saxony, Baden and other areas, see Emile Durkheim, *Suicide, A Study in Sociology,* translated by John A. Spaulding and George Simpson, edited with an introduction by George Simpson. New York: The Free Press, 1966: pp. 178, 183, 196, 197 and passim. Although Durkheim may exaggerate the significance of small variations in presumably fallible statistics, his book is imperative for anyone who wishes to explore further the issues raised in this one.

2. Carter and Glick, op. cit., pp. 347, 352, 355 and passim. See also "Canadian Mortality According to Marital Status," op. cit.: 5; and Kitogawa and Hauser, op. cit., pp. 108–113.

3—The Divorce Losers

1. Frank J. Prial, "Alimony, Child Support, or The Civil Jail," *New York Times,* Monday, April 8, 1974: 37.

2. U.S. Bureau of The Census, Census of Population: 1970, MARITAL STATUS, Final Report PC (2)-4C. U.S. Government Printing Office, Washington, D.C. 1972: p. 181–227 (Tables 7, 8, and 9).

3. Phyllis Chesler, *Women and Madness,* Garden City, N.Y.: Doubleday & Company, 1972, p. 328.

4. Jessie Bernard, *The Future of Marriage,* New York: World Publishing Company, 1972, Tables 6 and 28 (from Norman M. Bradburn, *The Structure of Psychological Well-Being,* Chicago, Ill.: Aldine, 1969: p. 149).

5. Andrew J. DuBrin, *The Singles Game,* Chatsworth, Calif.: Books for Better Living, 1973, p. 150.

6. Computed from data in U.S. Bureau of the Census, Census of Population: 1970. SUBJECT REPORTS, Final Report PC (2)-4E, *Persons in Institutions and Other Group Quarters,* U.S. Government Printing Office, Washington, D.C. 1973, pp. 36–48 (Tables 24 and 25).

7. Ibid. (computed from data.)

8. Hugh Carter and Paul C. Glick, *Marriage and Divorce: A Social and Economic Study*, American Public Health Association, Vital and Health Statistics Monographs. Cambridge, Mass.: Harvard University Press, 1970: pp. 347, 352, 355, and passim. See also:

Kitogawa and Hauser, *Differential Mortality in The U.S.*, American Public Health Association, Vital and Health Statistics Monographs, 1960 Census Monograph Series: pp. 108–113; and Canadian Mortality According to Marital Status, by Sex [and age group] (Death Rate per 100,000 During 1969–70), *Statistical Bulletin,* Metropolitan Life Insurance Company, August 1973: 5.

9. Carter and Glick, op. cit. Kitogawa and Hauser, op. cit.
10. "Canadian Mortality by Marital Status," op. cit.: 5.
11. Morton Hunt, *Sexual Behavior in The 1970's,* Chicago, Ill.: Playboy Press, 1974: p. 245.
12. John Bowlby, *Attachment and Loss,* New York: Basic Books, 1973.

5—Revolutionary Hayrides

1. Gilbert Bartell, article on swingers, reprinted in Lynn and James R. Smith, *Beyond Monogamy,* Baltimore, Md.: Johns Hopkins University Press, 1974 (read in galleys).
2. Ibid.
3. Ibid.
4. Ibid.
5. Ibid.
6. Ibid.
7. Alex Comfort, chapter on Universal Kinship, in Lynn and James R. Smith, *Beyond Monogamy,* Baltimore, Md.: Johns Hopkins University Press, 1974.
8. Lynn and James R. Smith, op. cit.
9. Gilbert Bartell, op. cit.
10. Brian G. Gilmartin, chapter on the sociology of swinging, in Lynn and James R. Smith, op. cit.
11. James Twitchell, chapter in Lynn and James R. Smith, op. cit.
12. Morton Hunt, *Sexual Behavior in the 1970's,* Chicago, Ill.: Playboy Press, 1974.
13. Ibid., p. 11.
14. Ibid., p. 151–152 and passim.
15. Ibid., p. 142–143.
16. Ibid., p. 263.
17. Ibid., p. 142–143 and passim.
18. Jessie Bernard in Lynn and James R. Smith, op. cit.
19. Lynn and James R. Smith, op. cit.
20. Hunt, op. cit., p. 213.

21. Seymour Fisher, *Understanding The Female Orgasm,* New York: Basic Books, 1973.
22. *Redbook,* January 1973.
23. Hunt, op. cit., pp. 211–213.
24. Fisher, op. cit., p. 195. Fisher found that "The greater a woman's feeling that love objects are not dependable (that they are easily lost or will disappear) the less likely she is to attain orgasm."
25. Hunt, op. cit., pp. 208–219; *Redbook,* op. cit.; Fisher, op. cit., p. 195 and passim. Hunt maintains that "There is no doubt that today more wives are having orgasm in nearly all of their marital intercourse, and fewer are having it rarely or never, than was true in Kinsey's time." But the evidence offered, combined with the *Redbook* and Fisher data, scarcely shows a statistically significant gain.
26. Richard R. Leger, "Painful Puzzle: Viral Venereal Disease Is Highly Contagious and Doesn't Go Away," *Wall Street Journal,* Friday, April 19, 1974: 1 ff.
27. Hunt, op. cit., 168.
28. U.S. Bureau of The Census, *Current Population Reports,* Series P-20, No. 255, "Marital Status and Living Arrangements": March 1973, U.S. Government Printing Office, Washington, D.C., 1973: 11 and 15 (Table 1., Marital Status by Age, Race, Farm-Nonfarm Residence, and Sex: March 1973 and 1970).
29. Ibid.: 11 and 15.

6—Single Menace

1. Kenneth Turan, "Last of a Breed," *Potomac,* Sunday, April 14, 1974: 16 ff.
2. Ibid.
3. Larry McMurtry, "Your Place or Mine: Speculations on Female Macho." *Potomac,* Sunday, April 14, 1974: 13 ff.
4. Harvey E. Kaye, *Male Survival,* New York: Grosset & Dunlap, 1974, p. 84.
5. Ibid.
6. Law Enforcement Assistance Administration, Statistics Division, unpublished data. See also: U.S. Bureau of The Census, *Statistical Abstract of The United States: 1973.* (94th edition.) Washington, D.C., 1973, pp. 152–154.
7. U.S. Bureau of the Census, *Current Population Reports,* Series P-20, No. 255, "Marital Status and Living Arrangements": March 1973, U.S. Government Printing Office, Washington, D.C., 1972:

11 and 15. (Table 1, Marital Status by Age, Race, Farm-Nonfarm Residence, and Sex: March 1973 and 1970).

8. Estimated from data in U.S. Bureau of The Census, *Current
Population Reports,* Series P-20, No. 223, "Social and Economic
Variations in Marriage, Divorce, and Remarriage: 1967," U.S.
Government Printing Office, 1971: 4 (Table E. Average Annual
Probabilities of Remarriage Per 1000 Divorced Persons 14–69
Years Old Married Once, by Age at Divorce, Duration of First
Marriage, Number of Years of Divorce and Sex: 1960 to 1966);
and 56–62 (Table 8. Average Annual Probabilities of Remarriage
Per 1000 Divorced Persons 14–69 Years Old Married Once, by
Number of Years Divorced and Other Social and Economic
Characteristics: 1960 to 1966, 1950 to 1959, and 1940 to 1949).
Also: U.S. Bureau of The Census, *Current Population Reports,*
Series P-20, No. 239, "Marriage, Divorce, and Remarriage by
Year of Birth: June 1971," U.S. Government Printing Office,
Washington, D.C. 1972: 8–9.

9. Computed from data in "Marriage, Divorce and Remarriage by
Year of Birth: June 1971," op. cit.: 6 and 8. See also: 48, 49, 50.

10. "Marital Status and Living Arrangements," March 1973," op.
cit.: 11.

11. Ibid., 3.

12. Ibid., 11, 12.

13. Ibid., 2 (Table B. Persons Under 18 Years Old in Families by
Presence and Marital Status of Parents by Race: 1973 and
1970).

14. Lynn and James R. Smith, op. cit.

7—Immaculate Evolution

1. Robert Ardrey, *African Genesis,* 1961; *The Territorial Imperative,* 1966; *The Social Contract,* 1970; all New York: Atheneum.

2. Elaine Morgan, *The Descent of Woman,* New York: Stein & Day,
1972.

3. David Pilbeam, "The fashionable view of man as a naked ape
is: 1. An insult to apes; 2. Simplistic; 3. Male-oriented; 4. Rub-
bish." *New York Times Magazine,* September 3, 1972: 30 ff.

4. James D. Watson, *The Double Helix,* Boston: Atlantic-Little
Brown, 1971.

5. George P. Murdock, "World Ethnographic Sample," *American
Anthropologist,* 1957 (vol. 59).

6. An interesting symbol of this shift is the decline of the old
fashioned men's magazines, with their emphasis on hunting,

adventure, and male group activities, and the rise of men's magazines emphasizing sex. Even magazines like *True* now contain articles in every issue on the general subject of "what do women want?"

8—A Man and His Body

1. Margaret Mead, *Male and Female: A Study of the Sexes in a Changing World,* New York: Morrow, 1949; New York: Dell, 1968, p. 173.
2. John Money and Anke A. Ehrhardt, *Man and Woman, Boy and Girl: The Differentiation and Dimorphism of Gender Identity From Conception to Maturity,* Baltimore, Md.: Johns Hopkins University Press, 1972.
3. Harry F. Harlow and Margaret Harlow, *"Social Deprivation in Monkeys," Scientific American,* November, 1962; Harry F. Harlow, "Sexual Behavior in The Rhesus Monkey," in Frank A. Beach (ed.), *Sex and Behavior,* London: Wiley, 1965.
4. B. Whiting, *Six Cultures: Studies of Child Rearing,* London: Wiley, 1963.
5. Steven Goldberg, *The Inevitability of Patriarchy,* New York: Morrow, 1973.
6. Margaret Mead, on *The Inevitability of Patriarchy,* in *Redbook,* February 1974.
7. Clelland S. Ford and Frank A. Beach, *Patterns of Sexual Behavior,* New York: Harper & Row, 1951.
8. George P. Murdock, "World Ethnographic Sample," *American Anthropologist,* 1957 (vol. 59).
9. Money and Ehrhardt, op. cit.
10. Corinne Hutt, *Males and Females,* Baltimore, Md.: Penguin Books, 1972.
11. Ibid., p. 73.
12. Ibid.
13. Ibid., pp. 52–56.
14. This is one of a long series of experiments and observations conducted at Yerkes Regional Primate Research Center, Lawrenceville, Ga. Irwin S. Bernstein, "Spontaneous Reorganization of a Pigtail Monkey Group," 111, Studies of Social Behavior in (Large) Enclosures. Proc. 2nd int. congr. primat., Atlanta, Ga. 1968, vol. 1, New York: Karger, Basel, 1969. Also, unpublished manuscript, Robert M. Rose, Department of Psychosomatic Medicine, Boston University School of Medicine, Thomas P. Gordon, and Irwin S. Bernstein, Emory University, Atlanta, Ga.

15. Patricia Cayo Sexton, *The Feminized Male, White Collars and the Decline of Manliness,* New York: Random House, 1969; Vintage Books, 1970.
16. Thomas Pettigrew, *A Profile of The Negro American,* New York: Van Nostrand Reinhold, 1964, pp. 18, 20 (chart).
17. Robert M. Rose, Thomas P. Gordon and Irwin S. Bernstein, "Plasma Testosterone Levels in The Male Rhesus: Influences of Sexual and Social Stimuli," *Science,* vol. 178, November 10, 1972: 643–645.
18. Ford and Beach, op. cit.

9—The Rights of The Knife

1. Alan Harrington, *The Psychopaths,* New York: Simon & Schuster, 1972.
2. Margaret Mead, *Male and Female, A Study of The Sexes in a Changing World,* New York: Morrow, 1949; New York: Dell, 1968, pp. 76, 77.
3. Ibid.
4. Ibid., p. 214.

10—Jobs Without Gender

1. U.S. Bureau of The Census, Census of Population: 1970. SUBJECT REPORTS, Final Report PC (2)-7A, *Occupational Characteristics,* U.S. Government Printing Office, Washington, D.C. 1973, p. 540 (Table 31. Marital Status of The Experienced Civilian Labor Force by Occupation and Sex).
2. Hearings before the Joint Economic Committee, Congress of The United States, Ninety Third Congress, First Session, *Economic Problems of Women,* Part 1, July 10, 11, and 12, 1973, p. 41.
3. *Occupational Characteristics,* op. cit., pp. 457, 461, 465, 469, 473 (Table 23. Earnings in 1969 of Persons 18 to 64 Years Old in The Experienced Civilian Labor Force, Who Worked 50 to 52 Weeks in 1969, by Occupation, Age, and Sex: 1970): and p. 486 (Table 24. Wage and Salary Earnings in 1969 of Wage and Salary Workers, 16 Years Old and Over, in the Experienced Civilian Labor Force by Detailed Occupation and Sex: 1970).
4. Ibid., Tables 31, 23, 24.
5. Ibid., p. 539 (Table 31).
6. Studs Terkel, *Working,* New York: Random House, 1974, Introduction.

7. Germaine Greer, *The Female Eunuch,* New York: McGraw-Hill, 1971; Bantam Books, 1972, p. 339.

8. Anne Steinmann and David J. Fox, *The Male Dilemma,* New York: Jason Aronson, 1974, p. 52.

9. Hugh Carter and Paul C. Glick, *Marriage and Divorce: A Social and Economic Study,* Vital and Health Statistics Monographs, American Public Health Association, Cambridge, Mass.: 1970, pp. 256, 260, 261, 262, 313–320, 402, 403 and passim.

10. "Roundup of Current Research," *Society,* Vol. 11, no. 13, March/April 1974: 10.

11. Margaret Mead, *Male and Female, A Study of The Sexes in a Changing World,* New York: Morrow, 1949; Dell, 1968, p. 195 and passim: "In every known human society, everywhere in the world, the young male learns that when he grows up, one of the things he must do in order to be a full member of society is to provide food for some female and her young."

12. Ibid.

13. Robert Martinson, "What Works?—Questions and Answers About Prison Reform," *Public Interest,* Number 35, Spring 1974, p. 22 ff.

12—Why Men Marry

1. Ingrid Bengis, *Combat in the Erogenous Zone,* New York; Knopf, 1972.

2. Ibid., p. 113.

Index

Accidents, single men's propensity for, 38–39
Adultery, 58, 61–63
Aggression, male, 87–88, 96–98, 101–5, 116
  perversions of, 121–22
Ailey, Paul, 29–32
Androgenized females, 99–101
Arapesh, Mountain, 117–18
Ardrey, Robert, 85, 87, 120
Austen, Jane, 8
Azar, Liz, 30

Bartell, Gilbert, 57
Beach, Frank A., 97, 105
Bengis, Ingrid, 147–51
Bernard, Jessie, 15, 16, 37, 59, 62
Blackington, Babette, 94, 100
Blacks
  poverty and bachelorhood among, 12
  Sexual Revolution and, 75–76
Bonding, male, 86–90, 120
Bowlby, John, 41
Braff, Ruby, 41
Brauer, Stuart, 67–68, 75
Bryan, William Jennings, 82
Bushmen, 86–87

Cambodian invasion (1970), 106

Cheever, John, 41
Chesler, Phyllis, 14, 37
Child-rearing, Arapesh, 117–18
Cleaver, Eldridge, 71
Comfort, Alex, 59, 72
Competition, 72–76, 78, 88, 91, 102–5
Crab lice, 64
Crime, 19–21
  See also Prisons
Culture and sex, 84

Darrow, Clarence, 82
Death rate (mortality rate), 61, 38
DeFreeze, Daniel, 115
Didion, Joan, vii
Divorce, 29–41, 72–75, 128, 153
  current statistics on, 5–6, 38–39, 73
Dominance order, 102
DNA, 88
du Brin, Andrew, 37
Durkheim, Emile, 22

Ehrhardt, Anke, 99, 100
Eliot, T. S., 133
Ellis, Albert, 59
Employment, 123–28
  statistics on, 12
Epstein, Joseph, 29

Equal Employment Opportunities Commission (EEOC), 13, 125
Estrogen, 98
Evolution, 81–91, 120
  killer-ape vs. amphibious ancestor theories of, 85–86

Female sexuality, 77–79, 90–91, 128–32
  man's submission to, 151–52
Fisher, Seymour, 64
Fitzgerald, F. Scott, 42
Flower children, wilted, 127
Ford, Clelland S., 97, 105
Fox, Dr., 31–32
Fox, David, 127
Franklin, Benjamin, 8
Frazier, Walt, 133, 135

Genocide Convention, 112
Gilmartin, Brian G., 69–70
Glands, sex differences in, 98–103
Glass, Byron, 69–70
Goldberg, Steven, 96, 121
Gourley, H. Wayne, 78
Greenberg, Sol, 36
Greer, Germaine, 71, 127
Greibe, Kathleen, 78
Griffiths, Martha, 124
Group sex, 57–60, 78–79

Harlow, Harry F., and Margaret, 95, 101
Harrington, Alan, 115
Hentoff, Margot, 56
Herpes Simplex II, 65

Hermaphrodites, study of, 94, 95, 99–100
Homosexuality, 74, 76
  statistics on, 16–18
Hormones, sex differences in, 98–103
Hunt, Morton, survey by, 60–65
Hunting, prehistoric, 85–87, 120
Hutt, Corinne, 100
Hypothalamus, 98–99

Impotence, 70, 75, 76, 130
Income, statistics on, 11–13, 37, 124
  See also Employment
Institutionalization, statistics on, 14–15, 19
Irving, Clifford, 30

Jencks, Christopher, 13
Jobs, 123–28
  statistics on, 12

Kaye, Harvey E., 70
Kayira, Legson, 1
Killing, as work of single men, 25–26
Kinsey reports, 17, 70
  Playboy study compared to, 60–64

Libertarians, 79
Lippmann, Walter, vii
Los Angeles, sex in, 42–55
Love, 89, 139–46, 150, 158–59
  See also Monogamy

Male bonding, 86–90, 120
Malinowski, Bronislaw, 89
Manhattan mental-health survey, 16
Manson, Charles, 115
Marines, U.S., 23–24
Marriage
  current statistics on, 5–6
  reasons for, 147–59
  trial, 61
  See also Adultery; Divorce
Masturbation, 104
Mathias, Charles McC., 106
Matriarchy, 96–97
Matrilineal groups, 89
McMurty, Larry, 69
Mead, Margaret, vii, 81, 95, 97, 117–18, 129, 131
Mencken, H. L., 147
Mental health
  "social involvement" and, 41
  statistics on, 14–16, 19, 37, 38
Mingus, Charles, vii
Money, John, 94, 95, 99–100
Monogamy, 61–63, 72–73, 77, 79, 90, 144, 148
Morgan, Elaine, 85–86
Mortality rate (death rate), 16, 38
Moslem world, 76
Mountain Arapesh, 117–18
Murdock, George, 97

National Center for Health Statistics, 15
National Institutes of Health, 64
New York City, mental-health survey in, 16
Newman, Paul, 29

O'Neill, George, and Nena, 59
Orgasm, female, 63–64, 78
Orgies, *see* Group sex
Ortega y Gasset, José, vii
Our Time (movie), 54
Oxytocin, 98

Parents Without Partners (PWP), 37–38
Perry, Frank, 41
Pilbeam, David, 86
Playboy (magazine), 40, 79
  1971 study by, 70
  1972 study by, 60–65
Prisons, statistics on, 14–15, 38
Polygamy, 76
Power, sexual liberation as resulting in, 79–80
Progesterone, 99
Prolactin, 98
Provider role, 128–32, 157–58
Psychology Today (magazine), 70
Psychopaths, 115
PWP (Parents Without Partners), 37–38

Quarterman, Joe, 9

Rape, 71, 75, 76
Redbook (magazine), poll by, 64
Rosenberg, Edgar, vii

Scopes trial, 81–83
Self Actualization Laboratory (Berkeley, Calif.), 58

Sex differences, 94–105
Sex roles, 86–91, 104, 105, 128–32, 157–58
Sexperts, 92–94
Sexton, Patricia Cayo, 104
Sexual Freedom League, 71–72
Sexual Revolution, 56–66, 71–80
   female resistance to, 78–79
Simon, William, 17
Simpson, Louis, 92, 160
Single men, general statistics on, 12–15, 17, 19, 66
Smith, Lynn, and James R., 58–60
Srole, Leo, 16
Stanton, Jane, 54
Steinmann, Anne, 127
Suicide, 26–27, 38
Sweden, 63
Swingers, 57–60, 78–79

Terkel, Studs, 118, 125, 141
Testosterone, 98, 99, 102–3, 105

Thurow, Lester, 13
Tiger, Lionel, 87
Tolstoy, Leo, 29
Trobriand Islanders, 89
Turner's syndrome, 100–1
Twitchell, James, 60

Venereal diseases, 64–66
Virginity, boys' vs. girls', 70

Walden Two, 78
War, 25–26
   See also Aggression, male
Washington, D.C., 1970 demonstrations in, 106–15
Washington *Post*, 67
Watson, James D., 88
Whiting, B., 96
Widowers, statistics on, 38–39
Will to live, 27–28

Y-chromosomes, 98–99